sandscript

José F.A. Oliver

sandscript

Selected Poetry 1987–2018

Translation & Introduction by Marc James Mueller

WHITE PINE PRESS ❀ BUFFALO, NEW YORK

White Pine Press
P.O. Box 236 Buffalo, NY 14201
www.whitepine.org

Publication of this book was made possible, in part, by public funds from the New York State Council on the Arts, a State Agency; with funds from the National Endowment for the Arts, which believes that a great nation deserves great art and the Witter Bynner Foundation for Poetry.

ART WORKS.
arts.gov

State of the Arts

NYSCA

Cover Art: Susanne Pannwitz and Juergen W. Lisken

Printed and bound in the United States of America.

Library of Congress Control Number: 2016960875

ISBN 978-1-945680-10-6

Contents

Introduction

„Caminante, no hay camino,
sino espuelas en el mar."
"Wayfarer, there is no path,
only a wake in the sea."
Antonio Machado

"At my cradle two worlds, in me two worlds,"[1] writes José Francisco Agüera Oliver in the programmatic introduction to his second collection of poetry, *Heimatt und andere fossile Träume* [*Homelan(d)guid and other Fossil Dreams*][2] (1989). Born in 1961 in Hausach (Black Forest), the poet is the son of Spanish immigrants who moved to Germany the year before his birth. However, Oliver does not see himself as a poet of only two languages—"poeta de dos lenguas"[3]—because German and his mother tongue, Spanish, were not the only linguistic spheres to influence him. The Alemannic dialect spoken in the region of the Black Forest, where he grew up and still lives today, as well as the Andalusian dialect of his parents, have also shaped his identity and his poetry. Therefore, Oliver's *linguistic* "worlds" are rather composed of two times two languages.

Commonly, a mother tongue signifies membership in cultural as well as national—or, in the case of dialect, additional regional—communities, which in turn are main points of reference for the development of personal identity. As a multilingual speaker, Oliver is at home in more than one place; he accesses multiple cultures, histories or national/regional identities. During his childhood, the multiplicity of cultural and linguistic influences were, for Oliver, initially nothing more than everyday life and thus normality:

"[T]here was a house that was two houses. Two houses em-body-ing two cultures. A house and two floors, two languages. Open windows and doors, hatches in travel. Arrived in the multifold long ago. The Alemannic dialect on the first floor, the Andalusian on the second. In between steps without grammatical gender. . . ."[4]

„[D]a war ein Haus, das zwei Häuser war. Zwei Häuser, die zwei Kulturen verleibten. Ein Haus und zwei Stockwerke, zwei Sprachen. Offene Fenster und Türen, Luken in Reisen. Längst im Mehrfachen angekommen. Der alemannische Dialekt im ersten Stock, das Andalusische im zweiten. Dazwischen Treppenstufen ohne grammatikalisches Geschlecht. . . .'"

The steps connecting both floors did not have a definite grammatical gender for him, since they are feminine in German (*die Stufe*) and masculine in Spanish (*el escalón*); young Oliver could not and did not have to make a decision, the language borders were permeable, the transitions connected flowingly. But later Oliver realized that the language, German, on which he was "turned loose" (*losgelassen*) actually "rejected" him, and "had to reject" him.[5] The "official" language of the German government came into his world(s) and destroyed the borderless equilibrium of his linguistic spheres. He is not a German citizen although born and raised in Germany. German law has permitted for dual nationality for adult EU-citizens only since 2007; Oliver could now obtain dual citizenship, but he refuses to do so. For too long he was asked by "official" Germany to make a decision, a decision that seemed completely unnatural for him. Thus, the "bilious green passport" identifying him as only a Spanish citizen at first thwarted the poetic potential contained "in this exotic as erotic relationship"[6] of his diverse linguistic influences:

> "Yet no poetry! Just sober prose.
> All in all I am left with two languages or two times two
> language scraps and a poet who started out to search for his language to
> not to fall silent, . . ."[7]
>
> „Doch keine Poesie! Nur nüchterne Prosa.
> Unterm Strich blieben mir folglich zweimal zwei Sprachen oder aber
> zweimal zwei Sprachfetzen und ein Poet, der sich aufgemacht hatte, seine
> Sprache zu suchen, um nicht zu verstummen, . . ."

The strict categorization of citizenship sobered Oliver's attitude towards his languages. Language itself had lost its innocence for him; he had to learn how it is used to define and defend cultural borders, to exclude by marking the differences and deficiencies of otherness. Hence, national attributions like German and Spanish became for him "abstruse" and "unfortunate" (*unselig*) terms,[8] bereft of the capacity to express his individual polyphonic reality and multi-coded self-formation: "German and still not German, Spanish and still not Spanish, on the move: Me."[9] Early on, he begins to write poetry and embarked on a search for words that could translate his plenitude of identities. Homeland (*Heimat*) and language could never attain any permanent or static status for the young poet but developed into dynamic and volatile qualities—into "temporarily matters" (*Vorüberheiten*).[10]

Monolingual speakers will usually only experience through their native language the assurance and certainty that will serve them as solid and unquestionable ground, allowing for a "natural" identification with one culture and one nation. José Oliver became a true poet of "uncertainty,"[11] always attempting to entrust himself to language, to rediscover his self in lyric, without the possibility of ever arriving at his "true" identity. Regardless which language he chooses, all that emerges are "moments in time passing (*Augenblicke im Vergehenden*). . . . And at times mere scraps (*Fetzen*) remain, adumbrating the whole. Instead they create whichever is fragile."[12] Oliver's poetry is full of neologisms that suggest such fragility, bold attempts to wring from language the ambiguity and semantic flexibility that are so rare in everyday usage. From the Spanish *la mar* (feminine gender) and the German *das Meer* (neutral gender) for example, the poet creates the neologism "*die* Meer*in*"[13] (feminine gender, "oceaness"), allowing both linguistic spheres to flow into one another. Here, the grammatical genders do not cancel each other out, as in Oliver's childhood memories when languages and cultures naturally existed next to and with each other. Instead, it is the limitation of language(s) that lead the poet to his border-crossing lyrical play.

Der Mond and *la luna* (the moon) are never the same for the poet; one cannot be translated into the other: "receives the white / night luna for me / like cold fever later the moon" as he writes in his poem, "Keep in mind, I am also a rose."[14] Later in the poem, the author finds the word that seems to combine both linguistic worlds by expanding the German term for the feminine gender of the Spanish word to indicate both spheres for a moment: "the mooness [*mondin*] / was oliveface shy."[15] For the moon, with its alternation between new and full, and the sea, with its currents, waves, and tides are not static but in constant change and in their shape only temporarily perceptible. Both *mondin* and *meerin* thus allegorically subvert the idea of "stable and distinct cultural identities"[16] in favor of a dynamic, process-related concept of selfhood and self-expression.

Today, José F.A. Oliver is considered one of the most "important poets of his generation in Germany" (*El Mercurio*, Santiago de Chile), and one of the most significant German-language intercultural writers of any generation. Hence, distinguished literary critic Fritz J. Raddatz declares: "We deal with a talent of highest quality, with a poet of entire individual dignity, with a writer of rare earnestness."[17] Among other numerous awards, in 1997 he received the *Adalbert-von-Chamisso-Preis* for his literary work to date. This is the most prestigious award for an intercultural author in Germany. German poet and translator Joachim Sartorius describes Oliver's work in the following way: "José Oliver's poetry is unique among the works of contemporary writers in Germany. . . . Anybody, who looks in present day poetry for music, for the linguistic and aesthetic experiment, for harmony between breath and image, for sound-crystals, will be amply rewarded."[18] His poetic style is influenced by the tradition of late modernist and avant-garde poetry—especially by Federico García Lorca and Paul Celan—and presents a plurality of forms and genres oscillating between short poetic notes "with burning stringency,"[19] text/media collages, dramatic poetry, long poems, and dense poetic structures. He exposes his audience to linguistic experiments unparalleled in contemporary German writing. Yet Oliver does not play with language in a consistent manner, which, in turn, is one of the challenges and joys of his verse for the reader.

His work belongs also to the tradition of German language criticism seeking to sensitize the readership to both the deficiency of language to adequately represent the experiential world and to its potential for shaping reality to its self-contained rules, to language's own "ideology" (Roland Barthes)—or to any ideology utilizing it.

So far, José Oliver has published twelve full length collections of poetry, two volumes with essays, and a volume on teaching poetry to high school students. Also a gifted translator, Oliver published his own translations of Federico García Lorca's work into German. Oliver's own work has been translated into Spanish, Dutch, Russian, Polish, Italian, Greek, Hungarian, and Turkish. Despite the wide critical acclaim for José Oliver's poetry in Germany, only single-poem translations are available in English. *Sandscript / sandschrift*, the first book-length translation of his poetry in English language, contains eighty-five poems that were selected from all his poetry collections to date, from his debut *Auf-Bruch* (1987) to his most recent volume *wundgewähr* (2018).

José Oliver's evolution as a poet is directly linked to the development of intercultural writing in Germany over the last thirty years. But what does this literary phenomenon mean in the German context?

EVERY WORD MADE OF WATER—OLIVER'S POETRY & INTERCULTURAL
WRITING IN GERMANY

Intercultural writing in Germany is as old as German literature itself: "German language welcome / as it behooves for a good hostess / well this thy foreign guest / who greatly loves your regard."[20] wrote Thomasin Circalaria (1185–1238?) in his didactic poem "The Foreign Guest" (1215–1216). The intercultural influence within German literature spans the centuries, from Adelbert von Chamisso, via Elias Canetti to Paul Antschel (aka Paul Celan) and further. Given the variety and importance of non-ethnic German authors in German literature, it seems impossible to define it as being simply mono-cultural.[21]

Even though literary articulation of migration is not new in the German context, the magnitude of demographic change since the late 1950s has created intercultural texts of "entirely new quantity and quality."[22] First of all, intercultural writing refers to a cross-cultural, multi-lingual literary movement,[23] whose authors do not stem from a German-speaking country or are members of first- or next-generation immigrant groups. The fact that these authors do not always (have to) write in German is often overlooked by both research and the literary market. Even (foreign) mother-tongue literature can be intercultural, especially since it marks the starting point of the movement in Germany after WWII when authors first began to write in their native language on their experiences as immigrant workers in 1950s West Germany.

THE HISTORY OF MIGRATION AFTER WORD WAR II

For the longest time, German mainstream discourses struggled to acknowledge the Federal Republic as an immigrational society, even though from the mid-1950s onward constant immigration to West Germany took place. The so-called *Gastarbeiter* (guest workers) came predominantly from Southern Europe to the FRG—initially recruited by German companies in their native countries to offset work force shortages—to work here for a few years, to save money, and to eventually return home. However, after a while many migrant workers brought their families to West Germany, too, and they settled and raised their children—many of whom were born in Germany—and a few years turned into many. Due to the assumption that their stay would not be long, economic and political actors did not create the necessary socio-political adjustments to allow smooth transitions into permanent residence status. The general population did not need to actively *invite* the foreigners into *their* society. By 1964, the millionth guest worker was welcomed, and by 1973 the national work force was 11.9% foreign workers (2.6 million total). As a reaction to the so-called oil crisis and price shock in the fall of the same year that put an end to the West German economic miracle, the government issued a recruitment ban for work-related immigration from countries which were not members of the European Economic Community (EEC). Nevertheless, the declining economy came in useful for those conservative members of society who had already brought up the *Gastarbeiterproblem* (labor worker issue), seeking to shrink the number of foreigners in Germany. With the exception of Italy, all other main countries of departure were affected by this new regulation. Until this point, the largest group of migrant workers came from Turkey (more than 860,000 up to 1973), followed by immigrants from Italy, Greece, Spain, and Portugal.

Before the ban, more than 600,000 labor immigrants arrived from Spain in the Federal Republic, among them José Oliver's parents, Francisco and Francisca Clotilde. They left their beloved Málaga in 1960, right at the beginning of the German-Spanish recruitment agreement, to seek better opportunities. More then two million Spaniards emigrated from Spain between the late 1950s and and the mid-1960s, more than 800,000 of them from Andalusia. Francisco was twenty-six years old and a hatter by trade, not necessarily a profession with a strong demand in highly-industrialized West Germany. Hence, the young couple did not settle, as most of the labor migrants did, in large metropolitan areas such as the Ruhr region, still driven by steel and coal industry; the Rhein-Main area around Frankfurt; or at Stuttgart, with its strong automobile industry. Instead, his parents decided to come to Hausach, a small town with a population of about five thousand in the central Black Forest. Due to its good transport connections close to the French border, Hausach's well-developed, medium-sized business and manufacturing sector supplying the car industry had already attracted a significant number of foreign workers—among them a small Spanish community from Andalusia.[24] More important however, Hausach was the home of a straw hat factory, one of the largest in Germany's southwest, where Francisco immediately found work. A year later, José was born, followed by three siblings, all born in Hausach during the next few years. Francisca Clotilde worked as a seamstress at the hat factory, and for some time as a shift worker at a metalworking factory. After the decline of the straw hat industry in the late 1980s, José's father found work as well in the metal industry in Hausach. In 1995, he died unexpectedly during a "home vacation" (*Heimaturlaub*) in Andalusia—after "thirty-five years of arriving in Germany, an arriving that has never arrived" as the poet recalls.[25] José Oliver's mother, his sister, and two brothers still live in Hausach today.

Most labor migrants, including Oliver's parents, stayed in Germany even when offered *Rückkehrgeld* (return money) by the FRG; instead, many took advantage of their right to family unification by bringing their close relatives to the Federal Republic. Hence, the hope of the West German government that many guest workers would voluntarily return to their native countries during the years following the labor recruitment ban remained unfulfilled. Since the Fall of the Wall, immigration to the now-unified Germany has increased again, with most migrants coming from eastern European countries such as Poland or Russia; many of them immigrated during the 1990s as *Aussiedler* (resettlers) if they were able to prove German bloodlines. Today (2017), after Germany has accepted within two years nearly two million refugees, mainly from Iraq, Syria, and Afghanistan, Germany's Federal Statistical Office, the Statistisches Bundesamt, estimates more than ten million foreign nationals live in Germany, about 12% of the total population. Additionally, 8.77 million German nationals have so called "migrational background" (*Migrationshintergrund*), meaning they are members of second or subsequent migrant generations. Together, both groups represent around 23% of present-day Germany's population (or 18.70 million).

THE FIRST GENERATION OF WRITERS/STORYTELLERS

Throughout the labor migration era, most guest workers were predominantly employed in low-paid jobs, often times with poor working conditions. During the first phase of labor migration, writers could be found who gave accounts of their difficult living and working situations in pre-literary, simple, and autobiographical forms such as diaries, letters, songs, or other narratives. This first voice of migrant authors chose to (continue to) write in their mother tongue (among them the Turkish writer Aras Ören) to sustain continuity in the "language they brought along."[26]

José Oliver's father did not write or report in any form or language about the challenges of his new life as a guest worker in Germany. Instead, he loved to tell his children stories from their homeland, Andalusia, and brought along tales from his time as a child and later young man in Málaga, as Oliver remembers:

> "In the suitcase, stories, anecdotes, faraway-tales that father unpacked for us only little by little, but which we then loved to listen to even more because we were after all proud of our origin which we children seldom understood, and primarily connected to the endlessly long miles of travel to the remote summer *heimat*."[27]

> „Im Koffer die Erzählungen, Anekdoten, Ferngeschichten, die Vater uns nur allmählich auspacken sollte und denen wir dann umso lieber zuhörten, weil wir doch auch stolz waren auf die Herkunft, die wir Kinder selten begriffen und in erster Linie mit den unendlich langen Kilometerreisen in die abgelegene Sommerheimat verbanden."

Francisco varnished his narrations with his imagination—reminding the children of fairy tales—but also with wordplay or puns, and the certain rhythm of Andalusian dialect, a "narrated Fandango," as Oliver recounts, "fragile links [*Gelenke*] . . . against forgetting"[28] deeply rooted in the Andalusian tradition, providing an imaginative anchor in times of uncertainty. In these moments, Andalusia came closer in the music and images of his father's words for young José, impressions that also had a lasting effect on his sensitivity for sound and rhythm in language.

Francisco Agüera Gonzáles' "narration rituals" (*Erzählrituale*)[29] were in Spanish with Andalusian dialect; only occasionally a German expression, pronounced with a very strong accent, migrated into his stories. Others, namely the "second voice" of first-generation migrant writers in Germany, including Turkish-German authors Yüksel Pazarkaya and Emine Sevgi Özdamar, chose to write in their non-native German language. But it took until 1979, when Italian-German writer Franco Biondi's cycle of poems entitled *Not Only Guest Workers' German* provided the programmatic grounds for the so-called *Gastarbeiterliteratur* (guest worker literature) as a new type of writing in Germany.[30] In this collection, Biondi addresses mainly the struggle of migrant workers with the German language, and the "disparagement"[31] by ethnic Germans of the so-called *Gastarbeiterdeutsch* (guest workers' German) usually with a heavy accent, deficient grammar, and limited vocabulary: "You bad Dago [*Itaka*], why you scream / why you bash German / why you so evil, so nasty. . . ."[32] It is striking in these lines that it is actually a native German, not the Italian, who uses a stylized form of *Gastarbeiterdeutsch*, but even more so that this speech variant, primarily signifying marginalization and discrimination, can be part of a poem. In doing so, Biondi appropriates grammatically and lexically deviant German as a means of artistic expression, both criticizing social exclusion and empowering migrant identity through linguistic difference. Along the same lines, Biondi chose the title *Gastarbeiterdeutsch* deliberately to positively charge a term commonly used to discriminate against foreign workers.[33] From that time on, their writing was self-labeled as political act.[34] Thereby, Biondi's poetry of linguistic difference broke ground for a younger generation of poets, among them José Oliver, further encouraging them to explore the critical and artistic potential in language deviation.

Nevertheless, guest worker literature in the 1980s was still also a form of *Betroffenheitsliteratur*[35] (literature of concern or bewilderment), as coined by Biondi and Syrian-German writer Rafik Schami, that sought to be a type of therapeutic writing by "victims" of the invidious social and economic processes they experienced in Germany.[36] Thus, it was part of a survival strategy. Beyond that, *Gastarbeiterliteratur* also defined itself as art by and for workers calling for solidarity between different cultures and countries in order to challenge the separation between migrant workers and their ethnic-German colleagues. It also targeted the German public to inform them about the experiences of labor migrants, evoking reaction and political involvement.[37] Shortly after this period, migrant authors and activists founded several writing and publishing collectives, such as Werkkreis Literatur der Arbeitswelt or Südwind, as a literary as well a political platform for numerous migrant groups in the FRG—"from tears to civil rights" as Franco Biondi described this shift from mere *Betroffenheit* to political activism.[38] Also in 1980, the nineteen-year-old José Oliver—who just started to study

Romance Languages, German Studies, and Philosophy at Freiburg University—co-founded PoLi-Kunstverein (Poly-National Literature and Art Association) with writers, inclufing Biondi and Schami, from twelve other countries. The goal was to foster socio-political change towards polynational culture and understanding. Therefore, before publishing his first book, Oliver was a political activist. It took seven more years before his debut collection of poems, *Auf-Bruch*, was published by the small literary press Das Arabische Buch, based in Berlin.

José Oliver & the Second Generation of Writers

The publication of several anthologies of *Gastarbeiterliteratur* co-edited by Südwind and PoLi-Kunstverein did indeed increase the awareness of migrant writing among the ethnic German readership. At the same time, however, it was also increasingly perceived as a more or less homogenous form of literature predominantly representing *Gastarbeiter* reality while lacking artistic value.[39] In reaction to this criticism against the activists' concept of *Gastarbeiterliteratur*, the PoLi-Kunstverein disbanded in the year 1985 with José Oliver being its last chair.

From 1984 on, Biondi and Schami replaced the term *Gastarbeiterliteratur* with *Literatur von Ausländern* (literature by foreigners), reflecting the growing diversity of migrant writing that further increased with now-emerging second generation authors, such as Oliver. Nevertheless, his activist background is, with decreasing intensity, still detectable in his first three volumes of poetry: *Auf-Bruch*, *Heimatt*, and *Weil ich dieses Land liebe*. In the introduction to *Heimatt*, Oliver writes:

> "My language is a rejection of the official language of a country that was and is not able to accept us. Through this act of refusal, our speechlessness is being defeated, and questions are being raised. Simultaneously, the language of our fathers is being challenged, and their way of life is mistrusted."[40]

> „Meine Sprache ist eine Absage and die offizielle Sprache eines Landes, das uns nicht anzunehmen vermochte und vermag. Durch diesen Akt der Verweigerung wird unsere Sprachlosigkeit besiegt, und es werden Fragen aufgeworfen. Gleichzeitg wird aber auch die Sprache der Väter herausgefordert und deren Lebensformen misstraut."

Language is for Oliver both the medium of exclusion through official or legal terms—such as *befristete Aufenthaltsgenehmigung* (limited stay permit) or *Duldung* (exceptional leave to remain) manifesting the only temporary and precarious status of labor migrants in Germany—and at the same time the medium for a resistance trying to give a voice to the unheard by poetically manipulating and appropriating German language. Additionally, the young poet introduces himself here as a typical representative of second-generation writing by criticizing the first generation of migrants for their hesitation to immerse themselves deeper into German language and culture. They mainly stayed within their native ethnic-cultural communities in diaspora while cherishing nostalgia and ongoing fantasies of return. During this early period in José Oliver's work, his writing is marked by an outspoken critical ethos expressed in more prose poems, scenic and dialogical pieces, and news/media collages all poignantly unmasking the strong bias against migrants and foreigners so prevalent in West German society. Additionally, some poems also address poverty or homelessness among ethnic Germans.

From the mid-1980s on, the first generation of authors also perceived the literary subject of migration increasingly as an asset and not only a burden. Aras Ören, in particular, opened the field of intercultural literature thematically by being the first to state that the Germans were as exploited as the Turks. Once beyond the message of concern or bewilderment, intercultural writing could tell stories of different homelands and multiple identities. But it took additional years for intercultural literature to be published with large mainstream presses and until it could free itself from the expectation of having to display a documental nature.

Since the 1990s, intercultural authors have been able to bring migrant writing closer to established societal, as well as literary, discourses. The intention of their texts was no longer primarily social criticism but a more poetic and aesthetic approach to social and cultural conditions—the symbiosis of literature and political activism lost its relevance. However, this does not imply that intercultural literature forfeited its political relevance, as we can especially see with José Oliver's work: the more explicit political criticism in his earlier poetry finds today expression in a more distinct and rigorous aesthetic form.[41]

Another crucial role in the growing acceptance of intercultural literature by the literary market, as well as a wider audience, was played by literary awards, especially the *Adelbert-von-Chamisso Preis*, awarded since 1985 to non-native German authors, among them José Oliver who received the award in 1997. Prior to receiving the award, he had published six volumes of poetry with Das Arabische Buch, including the 1991 collection *Weil ich dieses Land liebe* [*Because I Love This Land*] which, in a number of poems, addresses issues of German unification. A later volume, *Gastling* [*Guestling*] (1993), arguably his most political book, helped him gain wider critical, as well as public, recognition. With the latter collection, the poet comments on the changing conditions for migrants in post-Wall Germany, especially criticizing a new wave of racism culminating in hate crimes and violence against ethnic minorities during the early 1990s, as seen in the title poem, "Guestling": "Olor de muerte. / Siempre muerte. / To extinguish earth. / To set on fire. / Fuego into You. / Into You the blaze. / Cutover you. / The other."[42] Oliver's work caught the attention of one of the largest and most prestigious literary presses in the German-speaking world, Suhrkamp, and he was able to publish five volumes of poetry and one book with essays with them between 2000 and 2010. His arrival at Suhrkamp completed his evolution from a young activist-turned-writer to becoming one of the most respected poets in contemporary Germany. His success is reflected in the growing number of awards he has received since then, among them the most important award for an achievement in the arts in his home state, Baden-Württemberg (2007) or the *Basler Lyrikpreis* (2015), awarded for linguistic innovation "and the courage to [poetically] swim against the current."[43]

AGAINST THE IN-BETWEEN & MEER-KULTUR

Today, intercultural literature has arrived at the center of the literary market in Germany, though it is still labeled as "different." Despite its actual heterogeneity, certain issues are still traditionally assigned to intercultural writing, such as causes and effects of socio-cultural, economic, and political processes—the same positions that characterized its beginning.[44] These topics include emigration and exile, travel into foreign lands, encounters with foreign cultures, society and language, and of course the theme of personal and social identity politics. Moreover, a certain process-related, dynamic element as a unifying (but of course not always present) feature is recognized in migrant writing.[45] This relates to the rhizomatic concept[46] introduced by Gilles Deleuze and Félix Guattari that serves as a model for recurring structures and positions of intercultural texts that emphasize multiple and non-hierarchical representations and interpretations. Intercultural works in the German context often ask how dominant, one-sided "truths" about contemporary German society and identity, which are constructed around dichotomous concepts, such as *we* vs *others*, can be unmasked and countered through linguistic/aesthetic and literary means.

Indeed, to expect that contemporary intercultural texts *always* engage in discussions on these topics would erase crucial differences between authors, their individual experiences, and the aesthetic form their writing manifests. Nevertheless, against this traditional thematic framework of migrant literature, José Oliver's poetry seems to be an almost ideal representation of second-generation intercultural literature in Germany today.

However, he does not situate his poetry in between a dialogical position negotiating two aspects of identity, nor does his work mediate two different cultures or languages. In the past, Oliver has used the descriptive term *Rand-Kultur*[47] (Margin Culture) to position his poetry, as well as the writing of other German-language minority authors, beyond territorial, dualistic concepts, and to emphasize their membership *within* German culture and literature, although on the margins. Hence, Oliver refrains from using the term *interkulturell* in his essays. He observes critically that this attribute is overused, especially to label literature by minority authors for marketing purposes. Also Leslie A. Adelson postulates in her essay, "Against Between—Ein Manifest gegen das Dazwischen"[48] a shift from territorial, bipolar concepts retained in the construct of *intercultural* toward the understanding that minority writing occupies a position *within* German literature and not in-between or even (partially) outside, bridging, connecting, or combining two supposedly disparate cultures. Oliver instead coined the word *meer-kulturell*[49] as an alternative term to express the difference between members of the majority and ethnic/cultural minorities in Germany. The German word *Meer* translates into sea or ocean and is a homophone to *mehr* (English: more) as most of the immigrants who came to Germany from the mid-1950s on stemmed from Mediterranean countries bordering the sea. Their cultural heritage and traditions enriched German culture and society. With this neologism, Oliver avoids using the reference "in-between" (*inter*) with its negative allusions (detached, excluded, not belonging, undecided, etc.) commonly associated with ethnic minorities in dominant public discourse in contemporary Germany.

Nevertheless, one other possible, and eventually more fitting classification of Oliver's work is the term "transcultural"[50] coined by German philosopher Wolfgang Welsch, which replaces Johann Gottfried Herder's still widespread notion of national cultures as independent, homogeneous "sphericals," with a culture model shaped by mutual "penetration" (*Durchdringung*) and "interdependence" (*Verflechtung*).[51] First and foremost, the culture of one of Oliver's homelands, Andalusia, perfectly exemplifies the transcultural evolving of a historic place influenced through centuries by Castilian, Jewish, Arab, and Romani cultures. However, Oliver's German side is not homogeneous either, but laced with the Alemannic dialect and cultural peculiarities of the Black Forest region, which are in turn transculturally influenced by France and Switzerland. Equally important, he takes the transcultural perspective of his writing further and continues to travel throughout the globe. He is also concerned with poverty, exploitation, and exclusion of minorities abroad, such as in Peru, where he has traveled several times since the early 1990s, resulting in his volume *Vater unser in Lima* [*Our Father, Who Art in Lima*] (1991). His stays as guest lecturer and writer-in-residence in the U.S. (at MIT) and the U.K., his visits to Australia, or as *poeta laureatus* in Cairo

under the Midad project, sponsored by the Goethe Institute, have also cul-
minated in poetic travelogues in which he discovers universal themes in local
scenes and encounters abroad. The poetic results of his visits abroad are also
often influenced by literary traditions and/or by individual poets of the host
country, and "word troves" (*Wortfunde*) he collects at each place do further en-
hance the transcultural component of his work, e.g., in New York City: ". . .
breadrhythm / *sagst du* breadrhythm. *Ist 1 anderer / der brotrhythmus am textrand
der stadt.*"[52] These transgressions questioning and ultimately transcending
static geographical, cultural, and linguistic references, as well as his actual
(and imaginary) traveling,[53] do make José Oliver a true transcultural poet.

Despite its nearly fifty-year history as a factual country of immigration,
Germany's mainstream society still displays a lack of acceptance toward the
cultural difference of former guest workers—and today's migrants or Ger-
mans with *Migrationshintergrund* (migrational background). In the past, the
German citizenship law based on the principle of *lex sanguinis* did not allow
adult non-EU citizens to obtain dual citizenship, a regulation which espe-
cially hindered the integration of the significant Turkish-German minority
in Germany. Since 2014, however, young adults of the second and next gen-
erations no longer have to make at least a legal decision about whether to be,
for example, German *or* Turkish.

Nevertheless, in contemporary Germany, migrants of all generations
are still confronted with dominant public debates—mainly from the con-
servative side of the political spectrum—demanding a decision between
German culture and the culture of origin. Such dominant discourses ulti-
mately pressure non-ethnic Germans to recognize and adopt their German
side as "leading culture" (*Leitkultur*). An equal coexistence of German and
inherited background is simply deemed impossible by populist, mainstream
German society—a position that is mostly based on mistrust, as well as
general fear, of the foreign, and, subsequently, the alleged immanent *Über-
fremdung* of the country (being swamped by foreigners). Such societal reality
stigmatizes individuals equally influenced by (at least) two different cultural
backgrounds/histories as not fully belonging and accepted into the symbol-
ic space of ethnic German culture and collective identity. Until today, the
German government has ignored the increasing calls for a law regulating
migration—another strong indicator of Germany's struggle to accept the
status quo and to identify itself as "migrational society."

In 1989, in reaction to these non-satisfying socio-political conditions,
José Oliver formulated two interrelated poetic strategies guiding his writing

until today: (self-)foreignness and the pursuit of an "open language." In the introduction to *Heimatt* the poet writes quoting Franco Biondi:

> "Only when it can be made obvious that the threat has really nothing to do with foreigners and that it slowly reveals itself as vague fear of what one is still unfamiliar with, only then the chance exists to clearly experience that, in reality, it is the foreignness inside oneself. . . ."[54]

> „Erst wenn offensichtlich gemacht werden kann, daß die Bedrohung wirklich nicht mit fremden Menschen zu tun hat und sich als vage Angst vor dem, was man noch gar nicht kennt, offenbart, erst dann besteht die Möglichkeit, deutlich zu erleben, daß es sich in der Realität um die Fremde in sich selbst handelt. . . ."

In Oliver's lyric, foreignness is not associated with negativity, exclusion, or the need to be overcome. On the contrary, his writing is charged by the hope that rediscovering and acknowledging the hidden unfamiliarity with(in) ourselves as an unalterable part of any human being—a true *conditio humana* regardless of cultural or linguistic background—could create a positive dynamic between non-ethnic and ethnic Germans. Accordingly, their petrified relationship could be resolved by recognizing (self-)foreignness as both familiar and universal, ultimately leading to a more respectful encounter. Most individuals with migrational backgrounds are sensitive to their own inner strangeness; hence, it is especially the ethnic German side, presumably representing the majority of Oliver's readership in Germany, that ought to be reminded of their own innate unknown. Or as Harald Weinrich said during his Chamisso Award Laudation for the author in 1997: "José Oliver rejects any form of linguistic expression, in German or in Spanish, if it is not thoroughly exploring the foreignness 'outside' and the foreignness 'inside' oneself, or if it does not teach his readers to live in this world as foreigners and refugees themselves."[55] The lesson to be learned is to be able to encounter oneself in the foreigner—and vice versa.

Foreignness Inside and Out

The concept of external foreignization in Oliver's writing refers, for example, to exposing the audience to commonly overlooked positions of cultural difference in Germany. In this context, the frequent switching of codes, most of the time between German and Spanish, or German and Alemmanic, aesthetically represents such otherness, and will estrange Oliver's poetic text from the monolingual reader. Beyond that, increasingly in the course of his work, the poet takes his audience to destinations of his extensive travels— Egypt, Australia, the U.S., Eastern Europe—that are also foreign to him, capturing, in local scenes and encounters, moments of arriving, sojourning, or departing. Here, interspersed names of places, individuals, or surprising quotes disturb the textual coherence and further disorient the audience already on foreign ground. The results are dense, often polyglossic travelogues that "deterritorialize"[56] language, turning it into a dynamic space by itself for global travel and movement.[57] At the same time however, Oliver always inscribes himself into such poetic moments, thereby discovering and pursuing traces of his own identity—in which otherness is already deeply engraved. As a result, foreignness and familiarity enter into a dynamic, temporary, and thus unstable dialogue, deconstructing fixed expectations and stereotypes for and about what it means to be a foreigner—anywhere.

Nonetheless, the exposure of Oliver's readership to (self-)foreignness reaches even deeper. The poet confronts the reader with a language that is "stripped off" from all its familiarity and its seeming "automatisms" of sense and understanding.[58] He does not write only free verse poetry with very little syntax; he unsettles and disrupts fixed grammatical and semantic structures in search of hidden, denied, unheard, or lost sounds and meanings in the words and images he encounters. His later poems, especially, display a plurality of linguistic and aesthetic experiments: dizzying wordplay, repetitions, fragments and fusions, spaces, syntactic ruptures, surprising juxtapositions, colliding lines, typographical shifts and interruptions, lacunae, and much more. Oliver treats language like a *Fernlautmetz* (a mason of distant sound; the title of his poetry collection from the year 2000) and, for example, cuts words into syllables only to reassemble them again (e.g., *einkindern*, "child hooded" or *hörgast*, "listening guest"). The result is word-hybrids that often blur the boundary between written and spoken language, creating beautiful wordsounds/soundwords (*Wortklänge/Klangworte*) but also eventual dissonant tones (e.g., *furchtfalt*, "fearfold"). As a consequence, the reader's attention will shift from the content of the poem to the material character of words, highlighting the "self-referentiality" of text[59] and temporarily overwriting the referential dimension of language. Thus, even the sheer sound of words will take on meaning, a meaning that will not point beyond itself, but that is utterly ambiguous and will be free of any form of ideology.

But Oliver's linguistic in(ter)ventions go further. He inserts colons in words, laying bare hidden meaning and surprising semantic connections within familiar terms and expressions (e.g., *was b:leibt*, "what re:mains" or frequently *w:ort*, "wor(l)d"). Most of the time, the reader is uncertain whether a colon is meant to express opposition or unity of the "discovered" word dimensions. In his later work, Oliver also occasionally uses colons at the beginning of a line against their usual function to indicate a conclusion or to initiate a consecutive statement (": how we children counted the SNOW tears"). Such free-floating colons do not link the following phrase to the preceding one but rather connect the subsequent expressions to the experiential world, where it is the concrete experience of the speaking subject that lends meaning to words instead of language's own system of self-differentiation.

Moreover, José Oliver frequently substitutes the indefinite article with the number 1 (*1 luftholen*, "I inhaling") since both number (one = *eins*) and article (a = *ein, eine*) are almost the same word in German. Here, the author stresses again the materiality of language, turning the word itself into an object that can be counted or numbered. This way, the poet hints again at the actual reality or action represented by the word, its individual or even singular nature (here: one breath) usually hidden behind the word's arbitrary form that bears no absolute value independent of its context. Additionally, also in English the expression "I [one] inhaling" is more specific than using the indefinite article and gives the phrase a more individual character.

Apart from that, the poet also forms lines consisting only of "mighty nouns,"[60] coining ambiguous compounds such as *lichtalmosen* ("alms of light") and contradictory expressions, as for example *himmelsschutt* ("debris of the sky"). Also here, José Oliver takes advantage of the creative capacity of the German language and forms chain-composites out of several nouns (e.g., *reißbrettfiebersiegessäulen*, "drawingtablefevervictorycolumns") that, however, violate the standards of everyday communication, as well as of common literary practice, and thus, further estranges language from its native speakers.

PAUL CELAN & LANGUAGE CRITICISM

The two-fold compounds in particular will remind the reader of the work of another German-language poet who, as well, has a multilingual background: Paul Celan (1920–1970), whose poetry exerted significant influence on Oliver's intense and concise poetic style. However, apart from being at home in several languages, the experiences of Celan and Oliver are obviously very different. The suffering of the Holocaust—in which Celan lost both of his parents and was detained himself in a forced labor camp—are defining elements in his writing and use of language that is situated between speech and silence, word and sound. Being fluent in several languages—among them French—he deliberately decided to write in his mother's language, German, which was also the language of her murderers. With his early poem "Death Fugue"[61] he wrote one of the most well-known Holocaust poems to date, finding a poetic voice for the suffering of the Jews without trying to express the inexpressible reality of Auschwitz. In later years, Celan's poetry becomes more and more fractured and hermetic, especially through his increased use of neologisms, and here primarily compounds, such as *Himmelsmünze* (heaven's coin) or *Lichtzwang* (light-compulsion), reject easy, or at times, any understanding. He sought to let language pass through its own silence and answerlessness, "through the thousand darknesses of death bringing speech," enabling it to resurface in a condensed and "enriched" poetic form that defies easy and simplified interpretation,[62] as, for example, in these line: "Show-fringes, sense-fringes, / knitted from nightgall, / well behind time / . . ."[63] Considering all biographical differences, Oliver still tries to explain to himself his "gentle" (*leise*) connection to Celan:

> "To allow non-understanding, to listen ever deeper into the wor(l)ds in order to be heard, in contrast to all the patterns of explanation that also always mean exclusion. . . . Language effect and word effect that destroy: annihilate. How they—only in this way, I can make Celan's language against the silence after Auschwitz sense-able for me—*have* led to the Shoa. Not just 'led.' No simple past tense for the word 'lead' because the atrocity passed, not the time to live with it."[64]

> „Das Nicht-Verstehen zulassen, immer tiefer hineinhören in die w:orte, um gehört zu werden angesichts all der Erklärungsmuster, die immer auch Ausgrenzung bedeuten. . . . Sprachwirksamkeit und Wortwirksamkeit, die zerstören: vernichten. Wie diese–nur so kann ich mir Celans Sprache gegen das Verstummen nach Auschwitz ahnbar machen–zur Shoa geführt haben. Nicht 'führten'. Kein Präteritum des Wortes 'führen', denn die Tat ist vergangen, nicht die Zeit mit ihr zu leben."

Despite the fact that Oliver is not a German citizen and still is deemed a second-generation immigrant by German mainstream society, he identifies with the responsibility of the perpetrators' descendents to not forget the atrocities of the Holocaust. And, it is Oliver's awareness of the excluding power of language that lets him follow Celan's legacy like no other poet in Germany today, a power that in the case of Nazi propaganda had provoked the almost complete destruction of the persecuted other. For Oliver, rigid attributes such as *self* vs *other* based on fixed definitions are forcing individual biographies, experiences, and perspectives into ready-made categories regardless of actual dynamic life realities—especially in the case of migrants. Such static definitions are at the core of common and dominant modes of perception since they facilitate an easy and effective way of making sense of the world—or of ones own society. Hence, similarly to Celan, Oliver rejects an easy understanding of his work. In his poems, the act of communication between author and reader is often corrupted, the actual meaning is complicated or even "diffused," especially for mono-lingual speakers,[65] reminding them of Celan's hermetic style. However, Oliver would argue that hermeticism is just another (language-based) definition that does not do justice to his linguistic universe. All of the often-times irritating and puzzling wordplay and linguistic experiments seek to hinder the reverie of reading and call attention to language itself, unmasking its role in the production of meaning rather than in the expression of it. At the same time, the readers are asked to engage in a more active reading process: either to fill the "void" (*Leerstelle*) of understanding, the lack of unequivocal meaning, with their own individual interpretation, or to learn how to simply tolerate ambiguity.[66]

Moreover, ethnic/cultural dichotomies are not only linguistically produced and manifested, but are also linguistically justified: a main marker of ethno-cultural non-membership has always been a different mother tongue. By challenging the reading conventions of his audience, Oliver fundamentally undercuts the common concept of foreignness again: He estranges his ethnic German readers from their own mother-tongue, leading them into the realm of linguistic alterity and uncertainty—an experience usually only made by foreigners in a foreign language. With his language-critical poetics, the author seeks to create an "open language" that transgresses any "boundaries of homogenization,"[67] provoking multiple perspectives and interpretations on the part of his readership. Consequently, a poetic language emerges that rejects all forms of excluding stereotypes, prejudices, or other hegemonic discourse, a deeply political project that not only destabilizes common modes of perception but also criticizes a socio-political reality formed and maintained through the use of petrified meaning and dichotomous concepts.

With its linguistically sensitive poetic strategy, Oliver's writing follows the strong legacy of German literary and philosophical language criticism. At the turn of the 20th century, authors such as Hugo von Hofmannsthal expressed their growing unsettledness about what language can still express in times of rapidly-changing societies through industrialization, urbanization, technological revolutions, or the discovery of Freudian psychoanalysis. Other representatives of German-speaking language criticism are the philosophers Fritz Mauthner and Ludwig Wittgenstein, or the Viennese journalist and author Karl Kraus with his critique against mass media language in the 1920s and '30s and its instrumentalization by ideology and/or political extremism.

Situated in this long tradition, Oliver similarly dedicates his poetry to "working on language" (*Arbeit an Sprache*), raising the critical awareness for its limitations as well as its dangerous power with his audience. However, his poetry is never sheer criticism. His writing is infused with a deep and honest faith in humanity, and with the unappeasable hope of finding words he can entrust himself to in order to reach the other inside of him—as the inside of the other. So, José Oliver's poetry of "wor(l)d building,"[68] of transnational heterogeneity does not only critically engage in political discourses, it also offers far-reaching ethical implications for its readers, regardless of their cultural or ethnic background: it promotes universal societal healing through language sensitivity.

In any language, hegemonial structures and influences can be found, hidden in definitions, mainstream concepts, or everyday phrases. Hence, Oliver's poetry (in translation) also invites its English-speaking readers to develop a more conscious relationship to their language, to engage more actively—and thus critically—in the processes of reading, communicating, and understanding. Consequently, Oliver's lyric will raise the awareness for the resentments, marginalization of minorities, or racism promoted by and through words—as well as for the potential of language to overcome them —among his American readership.

BLACK FOREST & ANDALUSIA

Apart from his global awareness, José Oliver is also a *Heimatdichter* (homeland poet), a writer who is deeply rooted in his home region, the Black Forest, where he still lives in the small town of his birth. Many of his poems are driven by a desire to capture the beauty of this landscape and its nature, or the earnest character of its people. In his early work, he occasionally integrates Alemannic dialect in his poems, from a few words up to complete stanzas, usually in the form of a quote from a nameless speaker that often him-/herself cites common sayings or idioms. Yet dialect is not meant as a romantic tribute to the Black Forest. On the contrary. Most of the time, such lines express clichés against anything/anyone foreign or deviant, revealing the intolerance of the dominant society for otherness. Especially in rural areas in the south of Germany, dialects are still widely spoken. Nevertheless, one can assume that the vast majority of Oliver's readership in Germany will have difficulties understanding sections written in Alemmanic dialect since it is considered to be quite distinct from many others. Again, Oliver incorporates strangeness in the (seemingly) familiar. The reader will recognize these lines as German language without being able to completely understand them.

However, Oliver again expands his lyrical focus in embracing his other home, Andalusia, the home his father tried to bring close to his children. Through his songs and vivid storytelling—in retrospect reminding the poet of the rhythm and sounds of flamenco songs—he told his children about "their origin that [they] seldom understood."[69]

Today, José Oliver's poetry is like an "olive tree," as Rafik Schami attests,[70] deeply-rooted and branched in Andalusian tradition, but especially influenced by Andalusian lyric of early 20th-century poets such as Antonio Machado, Juan Ramón Jiménez, Rafael Alberti, and, first and foremost, Federico García Lorca (1898–1936). The latter three writers all belong to the so-called "Generation of 1927," named after the year of their first formal meeting in Seville. They sought to integrate Spanish popular culture and folklore, classical literary tradition, and European avant-garde writing influenced by Charles Baudelaire, by Cubism or Surrealism. At the beginning stands their shift away from a sentimental, subjective lyrical voice that could only experience a fragmented (modern) reality, to the dramatic world that should speak through poetic images, symbols, and allegories, materializing abstract concepts and metaphors. But modernity is marked by fortuity instead of order, it is cluttered with images that are "exchangeable and dubious."[71] To shed light on reality, these Andalusian poets made use of a poetic device that was introduced to their tradition centuries earlier by Arab poetry: surprise, as in Lorca's poem "The Interrupted Concert" from 1920: ". . . The wind has settled / in dark mountain hollows, / and a solitary poplar, / Pythagoras of chaste plains, / wants to lift up its hundred-year-old hand / and slap the moon in the face."[72] Surprising images and associations should, for a moment, unmask reality and give way to its truth, only to have the "darkness" return immediately after. Oliver's poetry is also characterized by surprising turns of imagery or associations, and by moments of epiphany that reveal a different kind of world than the one that seems obvious to us. But for Lorca the soul of things had to be reached differently. He and Antonio Machado proposed a stylization in poetry "in the manner of deep song," or flamenco's *cante jondo*, rather than a simple tradition of art directly copying imagery or meter, which was still dominant in Spanish lyric at the turn of the century.[73] By stylization, he meant using only certain formal features of traditional poetry, especially musical elements such as repetition or refrain—stemming from Arabic dance songs (*solea*), Sevillian songs (*saeta*), or of course *cante jondo*—together with experimental imagery and symbolism influenced by avant-garde poetry. In his works *Primeras canciones*, *Canciones*, and *Poema del cante jondo*, musical contexts, rhythmic and melodic analogies—all referencing traditional song—complement the image-based reflection and blend visual and auditory spheres into each other to create a dialectic between image and sound/music. An example of this is Lorca's poem simply entitled "Song" from his collection *Suites*: "Night here already. / Moon's rays been striking / evening like an anvil. / Night here already. / An old tree keeping warm / wrapped in words of songs. /

28

Night here already. / . . . ."[74] It is obvious to see how Lorca's example has inspired Oliver's intensive interplay of image and sounds in his poetry, as for example in his poem "augustvoll mond" (augustful moon): "eyenight keeping sight at the wind / in the windear / slurping oboe shores out- / side as I am / singing along / in the boughear mouth and sound / . . . ." In these lines, the perceived sounds and music almost manifest themselves in the rhythm and tones of the chosen words. Many other poems by Oliver also entail repetitive lines, reminding the reader of song refrains, clearly revealing the close relationship of his poetry to Lorca's verse, for example, most impressively, the returning Spanish phrase "jinete, jinete, la muerte" in Oliver's poem "Tentoonstelling II" that alludes to the frequent image of horse and rider in Lorca's work, which, most of the time, symbolizes death. Moreover, some of Oliver's poems carry a direct reference to either music (as in this collection, e.g., *lied haft*, "behind the bars of song") or traditional Andalusian songs in the title (e.g., *martinete*). In the past, he accompanied public readings on his own guitar or asked other musicians, up to complete bands, to join him in creating an intense sound collage of music and word. To the surprise of his audience, he also regularly interrupts his normal readings by singing traditional songs in Spanish, mostly lullabies (*nanas*) from Andalusia that had also inspired Federico García Lorca.

The Andalusian music and sounds of his childhood were immediate and fascinating for Oliver, but fascinating also in their foreignness since Andalusia remained, for the most part, distant and unknown throughout his upbringing in Germany. Yet once more, we find familiarity and foreignness entwined: Many years after he listened to his father's stories as a child, writes Oliver, he encountered such a unique tone again in jazz music by Miles Davis.[75] Accordingly, José Oliver does not solely search the world and language for music and rhythm in their harmonious, structured form. He seems more a collector of tones and global sound snippets and gathers, at times, creaking or crackling tones that create their very own inharmonious rhythm. Together with his word in(ter)ventions, he challenges his audience once more, exposing them to unheard-of sounds in German-language poetry, as, for example, a "slurping" oboe counters common listening expectations and experiences. Hence, rhythmic harmony and disharmony, as well, enter an unsteady relationship in Oliver's verses, aesthetically emphasizing the core concept of foreignness vs. familiarity in his work.

Lorca's poetry also plays with the notions of strangeness and otherness, with verses that often reach beyond the borders of sense and understanding. The traditional music of Andalusia that influenced Lorca to such great extend is, first and foremost, an oral tradition. These songs were handed down by generations of musicians, singers, and interpreters with each generation trying to appropriate any given song by slightly changing its content.[76] Over the centuries, many song lyrics developed into a palimpsest of text and messages, often leaving them without easily decipherable meaning, as, for instance, in many children's songs but also in other traditional poetry influenced by musical patterns.[77] Lorca, however, did not see in this lack of explicit sense any form of deficiency but rather a strength that allowed a deeper, more personal and emotional form of connecting to these songs and narratives. Thus he formulated that "the poet must reject with vehemence any temptation to be understood."[78] And accordingly, Lorca's poetry is characterized by fragmented ballads entailing narratives that lend many of these poems an atmosphere of openness and constant transformation. Both the pattern of fragmentation and the palimpsest of text have had a lasting effect on Oliver's poetics and usually appear in his work as intense text-collages combining multiple layers of parallel information.

Yet, Lorca's influence on Oliver still goes further. The Andalusian writer expresses in his lyric a strong feeling of the "otherness of nature"[79] whose foreignness could not be comprehended and ought to remain unknown. His hermetic and cryptic metaphors and symbols, his riddles without solution stand for the attempt to reach into the strange and unconscious—in man as well as in nature. José Oliver's work follows Lorca's legacy of expressing his poetic vision in a multitude of puzzling metaphors and symbols. In Oliver's poem "homenaje a federico garcía lorca," an homage to the Andalusian poet, his appreciation for Lorca's poetics becomes particularly evident when the Spanish-German author repeats, refrain-like, one of the most famous lines in Lorca's oeuvre: *verde que te quiero verde* (green, I want you, green). The color green in Lorca's verses commonly symbolizes a longing for an indefinable state of mind[80]: to a strange feeling of foreignness, which Oliver can relate to so well.

Finally, José Oliver, like Lorca, is also a writer of wonderful love poems. A few have entered this volume, such as "you speak" and "keep in mind, I am also a rose," both from his collection *Austernfischer, Marinero, Vogelfrau* [*Oysterfisher, Marinero, Womanbird*], which consists largely of poems dedicated to the love motif. However, the main focus of the selection for *sandscript / sandschrift* is Oliver's language-sensitive, language-critical poetry, work that goes hand in hand with his subtle awareness for societal and socio-political predicaments of foreigners and other minorities—in Germany as well as abroad. However, the central theme in the majority of poems in this selection is his own polyvalent Self, an identity that is neither rooted nor dis-rooted, but rather a "wandering root"[81] (*Wanderwurzel*), as he describes himself, with both foreignness and familiarity as its closest companions.[82]

When translating a contemporary author into a different language and culture, the question arises as to who his role models and peers might be. Such knowledge does help the translator to better position the work within the context of this new literary sphere, as it helps its audience too, especially in the case of Oliver, since this collection introduces him for the first time to a wider readership in the English-speaking world. His work is obviously influenced, as is other contemporary avant-garde poetry, by some of the major figures in English-language writing of the 20th century, writers who led their literary tradition into modernity and beyond. Oliver himself mentions, among others, Ezra Pound's imagism and Gertrude Stein's playful style as mayor influences from English-language writing from the (late) modern period. But there are many more traces in the poet's work linking him also to English-language lyric of post-modernity. Some of his poems, based on the scarcity of verses, remind us of the Black Mountain poets, who wrote in the U.S. in the 1950s: Charles Olsen's (1910–1970) poetics of "breath & body,"[83] which base each line on only one unit of breath (projective verse), or Larry Eigner's (1927–1996) focus on the "ambiguity of fact (& language),"[84] which created extremely reduced poems and non-linear writing. Also, the Language School of poetry which emerged during the late 1960s in the U.S. shares a similar language-critical poetics seeking to bring attention to language itself, its materiality and structure, ultimately critiquing the constructedness and passive consumption of meaning. Poems by, for example, Charles Bernstein (*1950) display similar strategies of disruptive and fragmented writing, preventing an "initial and illusionistic reading."[85] The lyric by Bruce Andrews (*1948)—another Language poet—exhibits a readiness for word experimentation that, at times, goes beyond Oliver's linguistic play. Andrews' word lists are often filled with breathtaking coinages, such as "lampix," "bliffles" and "baslurker," neologisms sounding like English word particles or suffixes searching for their root.[86] In a way similar to Oliver's, he manipulates the crypto-structure of language, often arbitrarily combining existing morphemes or simply making them up. In doing so, he aims to not only criticize conventions of meaning but to destroy them. In this context, it is important to note that because of a flexible grammatical structure which invites compounds and hybrid words from different morphemes, the German language makes it much easier for word experimentation that is still understandable for its readers. In Oliver's case, practically all of even his most experimental coinages still offer a basis for deciphering them according to the individual reader's interpretation of their ambiguous meaning(s).[87] The challenge for the translator is to find equivalents within the significantly more rigid semantic structure of American English that disrupt the reading process in a similar way, offer levels of ambiguity, and still enable (at least partial) understanding.

Another poet associated with the Language School whose work bears similarities to Oliver's is Susan Howe (*1937). Her poetry, as well, engages in discourses of marginalization—of ethnic minorities, women, and others—rendering their oppressed voices into a poetic language of "hesitation and stutter."[88] "What is silenced is not quite silenced," she says, and she writes verses that resemble Oliver's language in its emphasis on word sounds, and their enigmatic quality (". . . locked riddles gust / Early times / Eov and Ev / Land of anything / Forgotten preservation of / everything / Other prophets / Propriety Property / . . .").[89]

Nevertheless, only a few poets in American English make use of a particular sound phenomenon of language that perfectly fits Oliver's poetics: homophones, which the Spanish-German poet playfully employs in his work on a regular basis. In doing so, he takes advantage of their natural ambiguity that further estranges the audience from language, while, at the same time, sensitizing them for its materiality. One example of an American poet using a homophone to irritate the reader is from the poem "Iovis XIX" by Anne Waldmann (*1945): ". . . break here / & would a Walden be / set / round / with / caller / stone / wood a Walden / pre-historique / would / blue / a wald-man be. . ." [my emphasis].[90] Most of the time, homophones in Oliver's poems cannot be translated adequately into American English without losing their double-meaning, as for example with *Lider* = eyelids vs. *Lieder* = songs. One exception may be the translation of *Seiten* = pages vs. *Saiten* = strings (of an instrument) that Oliver uses frequently integrating music/sound with writing/language, e.g., *sprachluftsaiten*, which I translated into "wordwindnotes" using in the word *note* a homophone equally alluding to both spheres (to take notes, to write vs. a note used in musical notation).

It is striking, that the contemporary American poet whose poetics seems one of the closest to Oliver's writing today also possesses a multicultural background and came only at the age of nineteen to the U.S.: Pierre Joris (*1946). Born and raised in Luxembourg, a highly transcultural nation with lingual and cultural influences from neighboring Germany, France, and Belgium (itself a culturally very diverse nation), Joris' poetry is influenced by his multi-sided lingualism and displays many heteroglossia, *migrated* words that alienate the text from its reader (". . . Vier Takte vor K   time then   before / starting   a poesis that   keeps that other   that / began in bone arete   retrurn to turbulence   break / the slippery line   to work thanatos tetanos   Verkrampfung . . .").[91] Analogous to Oliver's writing, numerous nouns predominate his extremely fragmented, disrupted poetic style. The author, who is an eminent translator of Paul Celan's lyric into English, also coins compounds ("bloodroar"), and experimental neologisms ("unlanguaged"),[92] but not in such high numbers as Oliver. However, Joris circumvents the rigid lexical system of the English language, which does not invite the free creation of composites, by manipulating the number of space characters within one line. In doing so, he produces word groups in which the individual words almost blend into another forming quasi-compounds (". . . this homonuculus   frozen brass monkey   bone monkey . . .").[93] Nevertheless, as a translator, Joris does recreate Paul Celan's composites in English ("beamwind," "brightnesshunger," "latewoodday," "heartscriptcrumbled"—all poem titles from his Celan translation volume *Breathturn into Timestead*, 2014).[94] Ultimately, Pierre Joris seeks to disrupt, in a comparable way to Oliver's poetic strategy, the reading process to create plurivalent, puzzling, at times hermetic language collages. Joris' work, too, is a poetry of "crossroads"[95] and "nomadism" in which any static, absolute position or concept—in life as in language—must be distrusted.[96] At the core of his poetry lies as well a "processual poetics" of movement and change that recognizes the fact that "poetry is always another language, language itself already a foreign language,"[97] as the poet Jerome Rothenberg writes about his collaborator's work. It is again precisely this suppressed foreignness of the all-too-well-known that authors such Joris and Oliver want to expose.

Consequently, the translator of José Oliver' poetry must venture to achieve the same goal in the target language. One of my main emphases when translating Oliver's poems into American English was to refind similarly irritating and unsettling wordplay and linguistic experiments to alienate English-speaking readers from their language. The frequent compounds in Oliver's writing pose a challenge for the translator since this grammatical feature is not commonly used in the English language. Despite that, I decided to keep most compounds, even when consisting of more than two word adjuncts ("nightbluelightness," *nachtblauleicht*).

Another problem for the translator is the rendering of dialect in the target language. In the German language, dialects are very distinct regional varieties of oral speech that for most speakers not from the same, or at least a neighboring, region where a similar dialect is spoken are quite difficult (or impossible) to understand. In contrast, most American English speakers will generally understand the different dialects in North America, such as the Southern dialect, more or less well. José Oliver uses dialect also to estrange the majority of his audience from the text, again through the often discriminatory messages quoted from dialect speakers. A *geographic* translation of the dialect phrase "was de Buur nit kennt, des frißter nit" in the poem "das lied der sprache" ("the song of language") from the collection *Because I Love This Land* into, for example, Southern dialect from the United States, would have significantly mitigated the desired effect of foreignization with these lines. This would be even more the case for the large group of speakers actually using this specific regional dialect, who also might feel discriminated against by the translator's choice. Also, since dialects are usually particular regional, social, and/or ethnic varieties, using a North American dialect would have overwritten the German context with particular issues and associations coming with the specific North American context, and ultimately distract the reader. That is why I decided to transcribe this sentence into international phonetic alphabet following the standard pronunciation of the actual translation ("wɑt ðə fɑrmər doʊz nɑt noʊ, hiː wəl nɑt iːt," reading "what the farmer does not know, he will not eat"). This sentence quotes a very popular German saying meaning that whatever/whoever is foreign will remain foreign to most (simple) people, referring to either ethnic-Germans who cannot accept a changing society driven by immigration or again quoting a representative of the ethnic-cultural majority criticizing foreigners for not *adjusting* enough to the German ways. Apart from the fact that dialects are usually only spoken and not written, the phonetic transcription stresses the fact that Oliver quotes a nameless speaker's utterance; it furthermore estranges the reader from language without evoking particular associations unrelated to the original context.

Apart from that, I also decided to keep a few German terms in the translation to achieve a foreignization effect on the reader, especially since Spanish is a relatively familiar language to many Americans—much more than to most German speakers—and they will be less alienated by it. An exception for a German-language word kept in translation is certainly the term *Heimat* (as in "heimatless close"). On one hand, a translation into "home" or "homeland" does not necessarily evoke a similar extensive field of possible associations as the German word (*Heimat* could be a place, a landscape, a language, a certain feeling, and much more depending on the individual); on the other hand, one can assume that some English speakers are actually familiar with this very particular German expression.

Nevertheless, following Walter Benjamin and his seminal essay on the task of the translator,[98] one goal of *any* translation should always be to extend and deepen the *receiving* language, "moving" it to allow the original text to shine through. Accordingly, instead of "domesticating"[99] foreign meaning and aesthetics in the target language, I tried to somewhat Germanize American English, seeking to preserve some of the general strangeness the foreign language text poses to the target culture. My native language is German, and hence, as Oliver, I am not writing in my mother tongue.

However, this allowed me to write in American English from a similarly distant, less familiarized position, as Oliver does in his second language, German. Because of this, I feel I was able to take more liberties, to risk more in my translations of José Oliver's word experiments in order to recreate comparable provoking effects that many of his verses produce—verses that embody a "language of hope" as they are "[a] current page to the sea // not to decipher / the windbirth of sandscript / I borderline alphabet . . . ," as he writes in his poem "curonian three-liners" from the collection *fahrtenschreiber* (*tripwriter*, 2010).

Auf-Bruch
1987

Parting Tears

Fremd

von außen
suche ich Verständnis
für das Fremde

ohne
mich zu erinnern
an das Fremde
im Innern

Foreign

from outside
I search for understanding
for the *Other*

without
remembering
the *other*
inside me

Auf-Bruch

Wo sind meine Worte
die ich gestern noch kannte
wortlos
in wirren Gedanken
hafte ich
an ihrer Welt

ich vergaß
mich zu fragen

kenne ich ihre Worte noch

wo ist meine Sprache
die mich mit ihnen verband
sprachlos
in wirren Gedanken
hafte ich
an ihrer Welt

ich vergaß
mich zu fragen

kenne ich ihre Sprache noch

es bleibt ein Stammeln
betäubte Ohren
lähmendes Gestern:

ich sehe
die Blumen
ihrer Sprache
die ich nicht mehr pflücke

einen Augenwimpernschlag entfernt
ein lautloses Lied in den Rhythmus
de manos que tiemblan

Parting Tears

Where are my words
that I still knew yesterday
wordless
in spinning thoughts
I cling
onto their world

I forgot
to ask myself

do I still know their words

where is my language
that united me with them
speechless
in spinning thoughts
I cling
onto their world

I forgot
to ask myself

do I still know their language

a stammering remains
deafened ears
a paralyzing yesterday:

I see
the flowers
of their language
I do not pick anymore

an eyeblink of an eye away
a soundless song into the rhythm
de manos que tiemblan

es bleibt ein Stammeln
verlorene Zungen
unterjochte Kletten:
gezüchtet
fandangoverschlungen
bereit den Süden zu träumen

einen Augenwimpernschlag entfernt
ein lautloses Lied in den Rhythmus
de manos que tiemblan

und sie werden weißdämmerndes Dorf
una luna que se pone

und die Wurzeln der Zypressen
kastrieren und zeugen
den süchtigen Schrei

el canto que secuestra la vida
de manos que tiemblan
cuando la luna se pone

a stammering remains
lost tongues
subdued landcuffs:
forged
fandangointertwined
ready to dream the south

an eyeblink of an eye away
a soundless song into the rhythm
de manos que tiemblan

and they become whitedawning village
una luna que se pone

and the roots of the cypresses
castrate and procreate
the addicted cry

el canto que secuestra la vida
de manos que tiemblan
cuando la luna se pone

Andalusien

die Konturen deiner ach so sanften Hügel
sind schlummernde Zyklopen
die mich streichelnd aufschrecken

aus Träumen herausgerissen
reifen meine Gedanken
beim Anblick unserer künstlichen Liebe

der Traum meiner Kindheit
ist der stinkende Abfall
auf dem Weg nach Deutschland

Ich verhandle noch zäh
mit dem Schrotthändler blinder Gefühle
über den Preis unserer Eskapaden

Andalusia

the lines of your oh so rolling hills
are dozing cyclopes
who startle me caressing

ripped from my dreams
my thoughts ripen
at the sight of our simulated love

my childhood's dream
is stinking waste
on the way to Germany

I still bargain tenaciously
with the junk dealer of blind feelings
about the price of our escapades

Heimatt und andere fossile Träume
1989

Homelan(d)guid and other Fossil Dreams

gefangen

zwischen den dürren ähren andalusiens
und hagelzerschlagenen apfelblüten
hat pablo s. pablito
dreiundzwanzigjährig im exil
den kreislauf des lebens beschlafen

eine tochter gezeugt
geheiratet
die mutter

gefangen

zwischen hagelzerschlagenen apfelblüten
und den dürren ähren andalusiens
ist seine tochter
in den wettlauf des lebens eingeboren

die todesanzeigen lassen sich
nach den gleichbedeutenden mustern verschweigen

caught

between the barren ears of andalusia
and hail shattered apple blossoms
has pablo s. pablito
twentythree years in exile
spun the cycle of life

fathered a daughter
married
the mother

caught

between hail shattered apple blossoms
and the barren ears of andalusia
is his daughter
born into the race of life

the obituaries can be
concealed following synonymous patterns

weißt du noch, damals?

über den schwarzwald beugen sich
die hemdsärmeligen sommer
das gelächter gegen sieben
im garten nebenan war betzeit

die nachbarn feiern heute
einen jubilaren am vorabend
fahren die enkelkinder rad
ohne stützräder bereits

und die geschichten und die toten
streifen in die täler versöhnen sich
sonne und schatten in der arena
lebend kehren die jäger zurück

vor der dämmerung ein fleckiges abendrot

wie lange werden sich die blumen noch wehren
gegen das gelächter der gejagten?

ein blütenblatt ist vor meine füße gefallen

do you remember, back then?

over the Black Forest lean
the shirtsleeved summers
the laughing around seven
in the garden nearby was praytime

the neighbors celebrate today
a jubilee the evening before
grand-children ride their bikes
already without training-wheels

and the tales and the dead
roam into valleys reconciled
shadow and sun in the arena
the hunters return alive

before the dusk a spotted afterglow

for how much longer will the flowers defend themselves
against the laughter of the hunted?

a petal fell before my feet

heimatt

übriggeblieben sind
die gebügelten hemden falten
im gedächtnis eingelegte geschichten
und die augen die stechenden
der herren
die sie leichtzüngig doña nannten
manchmal señorita

übriggeblieben sind ihr
die haare ausgefranste fächer
die lust zu schlafen schlafen
und ein herzklappenfehler
wiegenlieder
manch spanischer trauerflor
und NPDwahlanzeigen

übriggeblieben sind
staubsauger geschirrspüler toaster
und ein mea culpa mea maxima culpa
vielleicht ostern weihnachten die heiligen
kinder enkelkinder
kochtöpfe und sprachfetzen akkord
immernoch mutterns hände

ab und zu ein rest lächeln

homelan(d)guid

remaindered are
the ironed shirts, the folds
stories conserved in memory
and eyes gimleting
of men
who lighttongued called her doña
sometimes señorita

remaindered with her
the hair, frayed out fans
the desire to sleep and sleep
and a valvular defect
lullabies
some spanish mourning bands
and NPD[100] election posters

remaindered are
vacuum cleaner dish washer toaster
and a mea culpa mea maxima culpa
maybe easter christmas the saints
children grandchildren
cooking pots and language scraps piece work
still mother's hands

now and then a rest of smile

homenaje a federico garcía lorca

mit leisen sohlen gehe ich auf dich zu
fast verschämt buchstabiere ich
deinen namen: f e d e r i c o
und deine verse: *verde que te quiero verde*
nachts
im zimmer
tagsüber
hinter herabgelassenen jalousien
atme ich
eine welt
von vorgestern und heute
fast verschämt
wie ein reudiger verbrecher
ein krimineller auf der flucht
mit deinem namen
deinen versen

morgen
federico
morgen
wenn es hell wird
werde ich auf die straße stürmen
unverschämt
und werde brüllen

vor dem ersten schuß

federico

verde que te quiero verde

homenaje a federico garcía lorca

on soundless feet I go up to you
I spell almost with shame
your name: f e d e r i c o
and your verses: *verde que te quiero verde*
at night
in my room
by day
behind closed blinds
I breathe
a world
of yesteryear and today
almost with shame
like a mangey villain
a criminal on the run
with your name
your verses

tomorrow
federico
tomorrow
when the day breaks
I'll storm out onto the streets
shamelessly
and shout

before the first shot

federico

verde que te quiero verde

Vater unser in Lima
1991

Our Father, Who Art in Lima

Im 16. Jahrhundert waren es Arkebusiere, die in unser Land einfielen und uns kolonisierten; im 20. Jahrhundert sind es Krawattenträger mit „James-Bond-Aktenkoffer", Boten des IWF.
—Alejandro Cussiánovich

wider besseres pilgern

mitgebracht:
keine rüstung
keine fahne
keine büchse
mitgebracht:
keinen hut
keinen mantel
keinen stab
nackt mitgebracht
ein lied
an mich an euch
mitgebracht:
keinen aktenkoffer
keine kreditkarte
keine zinsen
nackt mitgebracht
ein gedicht
an mich an euch
mitgebracht:
den willen
zu lernen
sprache

In the 16th Century, it was the Harquebusiers[101] who invaded our country and colonized us; in the 20th Century, it's the "suits" with James Bond briefcases, the messengers of the World Bank.
—Alejandro Cussiánovich[102]

against better pilgrimage

brought with me:
no armor
no flag
no rifle
brought with me:
no hat
no coat
no staff
brought with me, nakedly,
a song
to me, to all of you.
brought with me:
no briefcase
no credit card
no interest rate
brought with me, nakedly,
a poem
to me, to all of you.
brought with me:
the will
to learn
language

campesina

auf dem buckel dein kind
in der ausgestreckten hand
ackerfurchen brachgelegtes land
in den tüchern ausgetreten jahre
zum verkauf
campesina
aus dem offenen autofenster
mein nacktes weggezehr
dein abfall reicht nicht mehr aus
für eine handvoll milde
aus beton
im stimmengewirr der zöpfe
die gebeugten melodien
wir werden ruhe schöpfen
aus dem taumel der stille

campesina

on the hump your child
in the outstretched hand
furrowing barren land
cut and dried well-worn years
for sale
campesina
out of the open car window
my naked provisions
your waste no longer suffices
for a handful of lenity
out of concrete
in the buzz of braids
the bent melodies
we will replenish calmness
from the frenzy of silence

„Sehnsucht nach Sprache"
(in meinem gepäck ein gedichtband von Gino Chiellino)

sehnsucht sucht sprache
die eingeschminkten
gesichter fallen auf: ein-
gesackt die lust
nach lauten malerischen
dörfern Celan

sehnsucht findet zwischen-
sprache die kultstätte
fette
wird zur heimathure
rostet rot
nicht blau
in der einsamkeit des
pharmadirektors beim colatrinken
verrrichtet der kardinal
die notdurft und er-
segnet sich die kanonenfeuer
zurecht während
der abgeordnete
um stimmen suhlt

grunzt ein dichter
der / die / das
mit den schweinen auf
den müllbergen der stadt
suchen die ver-
zweifelten
häscher ihr
herkunftswörterbuch

fündig geworden
will ich fremd-
gehen
in meinen sprachen

"Longing for Language"
(in my luggage a poetry book by Gino Chiellino[103])

longing longs for language
faces in heavy make-
up stand out: sunk
en the lust for
picturesque sounding
villages Celan

longing finds be-
tween language the cult site
fat
becomes a homeland whore
rusting red
not blue
with the solitude of
a pharma director drinking coke
the cardinal relieves
himself and no-
blesses the gunfire
while the delegate
competes for vote
in mud

a poet grunts
he / she / it
with the hogs
on the city's land fill
desperate bloodhounds
search for their dictionary
of etymology

having found it
I want to go
estranged
in my languages

otra noche otra vida

abgegraste nacht
um erneut
in den tag zu
stiefeln
den sand
aus den hütten überleben menschen
papayafarben
die morgensonne
schleichende hunde
hähne
es geht wieder ans lebendige

otra noche otra vida

grazed night
to start afresh
the day to
stride
the sand
people survive from the huts
papaya colored
the morning sun
creeping dogs
roosters
let's get right to staying alive

nachts leichen die schatten

die eingefleischten süchtigen
durchkämmen die straßen

schüsse verhallen schier monoton
das streunende echo bleibt

mundtotgemachtes wird griffig
an hundeknochengerippen

nachts leichen die schatten
der hunde

querstraßenentlang
jäh umgekippte ruhe

wenn der trauermarsch der ratten beginnt
werden die soldaten gierig nach stadt

by night shadows dye

dead-in-the-flesh addicts
comb through the streets

shots die away in sheer monotony
the straying echo stays

the muzzled grows tangible
next to a dog bone skeleton

by night the dogs' shadows
dye

crosswayfollow
sudden tipped silence

when the rats' funeral march starts
the soldiers get greedy for city

eingezwängt
die soldaten in räuberpose
eingezwängt
die gaukler ins lächeln
eingezwängt
die verhältnisse auf polaroid
eingezwängt
meine zunge
das letzte geheimnis
vor dem ertrinken

restrained
soldiers in a robber's pose
restrained
the juggler caught in a smile
restrained
the conditions on polaroid
restrained
my tongue
the last secret
before drowning

Weil ich dieses Land liebe
1991

Because I Love This Land

vision in der nacht vom 2. auf 3. oktober 1990

die restauratoren rücken an
abrißfirmen bröckeln haß
aus dem gemäuer tropft gelüst

die alten schieben ihre jahre
vor die Quadriga Preußenkreuz

mit schmierparolen lausen Nazis
wie affen ihre köpfe

und Deutschland applaudiert erregt

aus kisten faulen fronbananen
trägt sich die habgier ins goldene buch

vision II

ich ernte
zerschnittene engelsflügel

und zähme
die beladenen würmer

wer weiß schon
um die gefräßigkeit
des letzten sieges

vision III

einbahnstraßen
die schienen schreiben
ziehen sich stunden
wie kaugummi

vision in the night from october 2nd to the 3rd 1990[104]

the conservators march in
wrecking companies crumble hate
desire drops from masonry

die-hards push their years
in front of the Quadriga Prussian Cross[105]

with smear tirades Nazis
delouse their heads like monkeys

while Germany applauds excited

out of boxes drudgery bananas rot
into the golden book signs greed

vision II

I harvest
cut up wings of angels

and tame
loaded worms

who really knows
about the voracity
of the final victory

vision III

one way streets
rails are writing
hours stretch out
like bubble gum

sparen platz aus
schließlich

für das weltluftschloß
aus regenblicken
und

kein ziel. nirgends.

vision IV

zwischen schenkeln blühen
die metallzeitlosen

angstschweiß treibt die wellen
hinaus aufs offene meer

die menschen hymnen
kriegerisch

vision V

herzzerreißendes lachen
durchschallt die mauerwende

feuer

aus schüssen krochen zitrusfrüchte
aus toten heldentafeln

leaving some space open
eventually

for the worldcastle in the air
made of rainy looks
and

no destination. nowhere.

vision IV

between arms metal blooms
and will have its fall

cold sweat drives the waves
out to the open sea

anthemic people
martially

vision V

a heartrending laugh
permeates the turn of the wall

fire

from shots crawled citrus fruits
from the dead crawled heroes' names

spaziergang am Rhein

uferlos die gedanken
der wind trägt vergänglichkeit
grillen vögel mittagsglocken

die sprache der vögel
ist nicht zu entziffern

das glockengeläut
streunt durch den tag
der wind schleppt zeit

a walk along the Rhein

shoreless the thoughts
wind carries transience
crickets birds bells at noon

the language of birds
is indecipherable

the bells' ringing
strays through the day
wind is dragging time

das lied der sprache

ich habe gelernt
das wort **liebe**
den satz
zärtlich umarme ich dich
gefühlt gespürt empfunden

ich habe gelernt
das wort **sehnsucht**
den satz
ich will mit dir verschmelzen
gefühlt gespürt empfunden

ich habe gelernt
das wort **freund**
den satz
gib mir mut zum anderssein
gefühlt gespürt empfunden

heute morgen erst
hat wieder ein mann
kaffee aufgebrüht
mit seinem hund gefrühstückt
auf einem sofa eingesackt
in irgendeinem wohnzimmer
die vergangenheit herausgekramt
und sich der frage nicht gestellt
**„Warum nur bin ich gekommen
in dieses Land?"**

dabei lag die tageszeitung
ganz unscheinbar selbstverständlich
selbstverständlich
auf dem küchentisch
und hat buchstabiert das wort **Ausländergesetz**
den satz
Deutschland den Deutschen

the song of language

I have learned
the word **love**
the sentence
tenderly I embrace you
felt touched tasted them

I have learned
the word **longing**
the sentence
I want to melt into you
felt touched tasted them

I have learned
the word **friend**
the sentence
give me the courage to be different
felt touched tasted them

just this morning
again a man
brewed some coffee
had breakfast with his dog
sunken on a sofa
in a random living room
dug out the past
and did not face the question
**"But why did I come
to this land?"**

although the newspaper lay
all inconspicuous naturally
natural
on the kitchen table
and has spelled the word **Foreigners Law**
the sentence
Germany for the Germans

ich habe gelernt
das wort **haß**
den satz
was de Buur nit kennt, des frißter nit
gefühlt gespürt empfunden

ich habe gelernt
das wort **demut**
den satz
der mensch haßt einsam
gefühlt gespürt empfunden

trage einen mann in mir
ein frühstück einen hund
eine tageszeitung und ein sofa
gelächter tod vergangenheit
und erlebe meine sprachen

(für Francisco A., der sich jeden Tag auf einem Sofa
Geschichten erzählt aus seiner Jugend, um die Inventur-
liste seiner Wanderung abzuschließen
und für den unbekannten Obdachlosen, der jede Nacht
in der Charlottenpassage in Stuttgart auf den kalten
Fliesen schläft, seine graue Jacke übers Gesicht gezogen)

I have learned
the word hate
the sentence
wɑt ðə fɑrmər doʊz nɑt noʊ, hiː wəl nɑt iːt
felt touched tasted them

I have learned
the word **humbleness**
the sentence
man hates solitarily
felt touched tasted them

I carry a man inside
a breakfast a dog
a newspaper and a sofa
laughter death a past
and live through my languages

(for Francisco A. who on a sofa everyday
tells stories to himself from his youth in order to
complete the inventory-list of his migration,
and for the homeless man without name who every night
in the Charlotten Arcade in Stuttgart sleeps on cold tiles,
his jacket pulled over his face)

los caminos – die Wege
ein Zyklus für Gisela

I
los caminos son
sind die wege
zufällig vergebungen
vagabunden

auch einblick
ins gelobte land

ein lächeln demut
ohne muschel ohne segen

II
das fleisch
die knochen

müde fallen
vergiftete wiesen

III
lächeln unter hausarrest
weiße rosen blühen nähe

mein hirn wird wortgehäuse
mit kristallenem gerippe

IV
blick ins wasser
geronnene erde

aufgeworfen knochen
abgeworfen ein gebet

los caminos – the Roads
a Cycle for Gisela

I
los caminos son
are the roads
by accident absolutions
vagabonds

also the promised land
insight

a smile humility
neither sea shell nor benison

II
the flesh
the bones

wearily falling
poisoned meadows

III
smile under house arrest
white roses flourish closeness

my brain becoming wordcage
with crystalline skeleton

IV
glance into the water
clotted earth

banked up bones
a prayer is dropped down

dein blick stillt durst
ein kinderlächeln

V
ein höllenfenster tut sich auf
ein stein gemacht
zerfällt zermürbt
die farben kehren heim

auf den wegen der kastanien
fallen engel häuser
die knochen tragen trauer
nach dem verrat der bomben

VI
mein atem
hauch zerbröckelt

eine zehenspitze erde

VII
eingebrochen in die erde
lichtstrahl warm

so irdisch eingetauft
lebenstaucher blut

VIII
land/schaft

der geschorenen toten
umgeschorene knochenerde

your eye quenches thirst
the smile of a child

V
windows of hell looming large
a stone made
comes asunder worn down
the colors return home

on the roads of chestnuts
falling angels houses
the bones wear black
after the bombs' betrayal

VI
my breath
of air crumbles

one tiptoe of earth

VII
broken through the ground
lightbeam warm

so worldly wholy bathed
lifediver blood

VIII
land/scape

of the shorn dead
shorn bone ashes tilled

noch tiefer grübeln

zum zarten fell geborgenheit

IX
ich sammle ein:

schmetterlinge flügelschläge
sarkophag um sarkophag

in zarten blicken
trinke ich

X
und dann

so plötzlich

die lust
zu streicheln

die überreste
verschlossenen türen

mauerwerke
die verwesen

XI
der teufel spricht

unter dem schlangenbaum
brütet Adam eier aus
und Eva hackt die felder

pondering even deeper

to the frail skin of feeling safe

IX
I gather:

butterflies wingbeats
sarcophagus after sarcophagus

in tender gazes
I drink

X
and then

so sudden

the desire
to caress

the remnants
closed doors

stoneworks
being in decay

XI
the devil speaks

and beneath the serpent's tree
Adam hatches eggs
and Eva hoeing fields

sieben an der zahl
gefallene engel

XII
mein lächeln trinkt frieden
in deinem mund

wir schöpfen tage
aus maisblütenklängen

seven in number
fallen angels

XII
my smile drinks peace
in your mouth

we drank & cre/ate days
from cornflowersounds

DIALEKTIK

einen ganzen nachmittag
lang
hatte ich über die
vollkommenheit
des menschen nachgedacht

schließlich legte ich
eine schallplatte auf

die Unvollendete
von Schubert

ich war hingerissen

DIALECTIC

one whole afternoon
long
I had thought
about the completeness
of man

finally I played
a record

the Unfinished Symphony
by Schubert

I was enruptured

friedensgebet

gerstenfelder algengrüne
schräg gegenüber
der wind webt lebensmuster
über die hänge
rotgebeugt sträuben sich
tannen fichten noch

taubentappen auf den dächern

der tag sät taubenfedern
leichen sind vom himmel
gefallene kadaver
die bauern halten totenschmaus

ums nächtliche feuer
erzählen die alten die jungen
von der einen weißen legende

unter den trauergästen
weilt der frieden

herzzerreißendes gelächter

prayer for peace

barleyfields algeagreen
cater-cornered
the wind weaves patterns of life
over hillsides
redbent forward writhe
still firs spruces

pigeon pitter-patter on the roofs

the day seeds pigeon feathers
corpses are carcasses
fallen from the sky
the peasants take their funeral feast

around the nightly fire
tell the old and young
of the one white legend

among the mourners
lingers peace

heartrending laughter

Gastling
1993

Guestling

angezählt

ins land geboren
zufällig eins
entzweit
angekommen
aufgebrochen

gastling

counted down

born into this land
one by chance
parted
arrived
torn again

guestling

Poem eines mir anvertrauten Gastlings

Despierto.
De madrugada despierto.
Despierto los anhelos.
Es la noche que llega.
Su mano de fuego.
Llega a tocar las puertas de mis casas.
La despierto.
Mano que busca el olor del olvido.
Olvido transparente.
Velos fugitivos.
Las aguas.
Su memoria.
Oh, pardon...
Ich vergaß,
daß ich in Deutschland bin.

Ich wache auf.
Es scheint Nacht zu sein.
Nachts wache ich auf.
Noch bevor ich zu Bett gegangen,
eingeschlafen bin,
wache ich auf.
Noch bevor mir die Dämmerung zuvorkommen kann,
der Morgen.
Despierto.
La despierto.
La noche.
Ein letztes Mal.
Die Atemzüge zu zählen.
Die Atemzüge.
Leise Stimmen.
Erstickendes Flüstern.
Die fliehenden Atemzüge.
Dies seltsame Aufwachen.
Dies abgeschnittene Aufwachen.
Entlegene Seitentäler zu hören.
Dies Aufwachen der Atemzüge.

Poem of a Guestling entrusted to me

Despierto.
De madrugada despierto.
Despierto los anhelos.
Es la noche que llega.
Su mano de fuego.
Llega a tocar las puertas de mis casas.
La despierto.
Mano que busca el olor del olvido.
Olvido transparente.
Velos fugitivos.
Las aguas.
Su memoria.
Oh, pardon...
I forgot,
that I am in Germany.

I wake up.
It seems to be night.
At night I wake up.
Even before I have gone to bed
and fallen asleep,
I wake up.
Even before dawn could beat me to it,
the morning.
Despierto.
La despierto.
La noche.
For the last time.
To count the breaths of air.
The breaths of air.
Soft voices.
Smothering whispering.
Breaths of air escaping.
This strange waking up.
This cut off waking up.
To hear side valleys, remote.
This waking up of breaths.

Atemzüge wie Rufende.
Vertriebenes Aufwachen,
das sich belauert.
Ertapptes Aufwachen.
Ein Aufwachen auf der Flucht.

Schattenhäute schließlich,
die erfangen werden.
Leibgeding des Atems.
Eigen.
Dann bin ich den Türen nah.
Türen zum Nicht-Haus Haus.
Haus der bereiten Türen.
Dann gehöre ich dem Exil.
Ganz.
Ich gehöre den Umrissen eines Körpers,
der geht.
Für immer geht.
Es ist ein Aufwachen ohne Rückkehr.
Ein Aufwachen,
wie man nur in Deutschland aufwachen kann.
Wie man in Deutschland aufwachen muß.
Wie man gezwungen wird,
in Deutschland aufzuwachen.
Wie man gezwungen wird,
in Deutschland aufzuwachen,
wenn man in diesem Land geboren wurde,
aber nie dazugehören durfte.
Wie man nie geboren wurde
und deshalb dazugehört.
Ein nichterlaubtes Aufwachen.
Es ist dein Aufwachen in Deutschland.
Überall dort,
wo Deutschland ist.
Überall dort,
wo Deutschland Deutschland ist.
Dann braucht die Nacht eine Übersetzerin.

Breaths of air like shouters.
An expulsed waking up,
that stalks itself.
Caught out waking up.
A waking up on the run.

Shadowskins, after all,
that are caught on.
Heartwork of breathing.
Mine and foreign.
Then I can almost touch the doors.
Doors to the non-house house.
House of the wiped doors.
Then the exile possesses me.
Entirely.
The silhouette of a body
that leaves possesses me.
Ever leaving.
It is a waking up without return.
A waking up
as you can wake up only in Germany.
As you have to wake up in Germany.
As you are forced
to wake up in Germany.
As you are forced
to wake up in Germany
when you were born in this country
but could never belong.
As you were never born
and therefore belong on these grounds.
A non-permitted waking up.
It is Your waking up in Germany.
In all places
where Germany is.
In all places
where Germany Germany is.
Then the night needs a female translator.

Wortmalerin,
Haut nachzudichten.
Entfernte.
Dann braucht die Nacht eine Sprache,
die nicht in Worten bestehen könnte.
Farbenlaute.
Gedächtnis,
mein durchsichtiges Vergessen.
Transparente Erinnerung.
So schafft sich die Nacht ihr Attentat.
Kleine Morde.
Hinterrücks.

Die Nacht braucht also einen Geruch.
Die Nacht braucht ihren Geruch.
Ich kenne diesen Geruch.
Ich wache auf
und fühle mich diesen Geruch hören.
Einkindern.
So lernt man Gehorsam.
Geruch der alten Erzählungen.
Begebenheiten,
die sich verbünden.
Notschlachtungen.
Wie Kriegsveteranen.
Wie Fronten nach dem Gelächter.
Verbündete des Vergessens.
Schweigen der Liebenden vor dem Gehen.
Tätowiertes Schweigen.
Hautschweigen.
Dies Leben hin zum Vergessen.
Gerodete Stille.
Es riecht nach Schweigen.
Es riecht nach abgelegten Tagen.
Das Schweigen.
Seine Geschichte,
vernarbte Zärtlichkeit.

A wordpaintress
to reversify skin.
The removed one.
Then the night needs a language
that could not be made of words.
Colorsounds.
Memory,
my clear forgetting.
Transparent remembering.
This way the night creates her assassination.
Small murders.
From behind.

So the night needs a scent.
The night needs her scent.
I know this scent.
I wake up
and feel myself hearing this scent.
Child hooded.
This is how you learn obedience.
Scent of the old tales.
Occurrences
that ally themselves.
Emergency slaughterings.
Like war veterans.
Like front lines after the laughs.
Allies of oblivion.
Silence of the lovers before leaving.
Tattooed silence.
Skinsilence.
This life into oblivion.
Felled calmness.
It smells of silence.
It smells of abandoned days.
The silence.
Its history,
scarred tenderness.

Der Geruch ist ihr Liebhaber,
den man verlassen hat.
Den man verlassen mußte.
Den man immer verlassen muß.

Der Geruch ist der Geruch Spaniens.
Erlegtes Spanien nach der Belagerung,
so wie ich Andalusien roch.
Wie nur ich Andalusien riechen konnte.
Wie ich Andalusien riechen mußte.
Wie ich irgendwann gezwungen war,
Andalusien zu riechen.
Wie man gezwungen war,
Andalusien zu riechen,
wenn man nicht dort geboren wurde
und dazugehören mußte.
Wie man immer geboren wird
und nicht dazu gehört.

Der Geruch ist also Andalusien.
Überall dort,
wo Andalusien ist.
So wegtauschbar.
Überall dort,
wo Andalusien Andalusien ist.
Auchtür zur Fremde.

Der Geruch war die Fremde.
Ist die Fremde,
die bleibt.
Ihr Spaziergang.
Die Fremde,
die man erkennt,
begeht.
Nachmittage.
Die kleinen Morde.
Anatolien in Augen.

The scent is her lover
who was left alone.
Who had to be left alone.
Who always has to be left alone.

This scent is the scent of Spain.
Hunted down Spain after the siege,
this is how I smelled Andalusia.
How only I could smell Andalusia.
Andalusia, how I had to smell it.
How you were forced one day
to smell Andalusia.
How you were forced
to smell Andalusia
if you were not born there
and had to belong.
As you are always born
but do not belong.

So, Andalusia is the scent.
In all places
where Andalusia is.
So misplaceable.
In all places
where Andalusia Andalusia is.
Alter door to the foreign.

The scent was the foreign.
Is the foreign
that stays.
Her promenade.
The foreign
that one recognizes,
passes through.
Afternoons.
The little murders.
Anatolia in eyes.

Das Gehör der Ränder.
Klänge auszufransen.
Wie ein sizilianisches Lied.
Eine Bauernhochzeit.
Schlesien nach der Wanderung.
Ein Zugvogel.
Nach Böhmen.
Nach Patagonien.

Die Fremde hat also ihren Geruch.
Straßenzüge.
Überall Buenos Aires.
Fadengehaltenes Buenos Aires.
Die Lieder.
Melancholie.
Die Närrin.
Die Übersetzerin.
Quer übers Gesicht.
Ein fliehendes Bandoleon.
Draußen vor dem Tod.
Diese Finger.
Diese kalten Finger.
Danach.

Despierto.
La despierto.
Die Nacht hat also ein Gesicht.
Ihr Gesicht,
ein Geruch.
Das Gesicht ist ein Überfall
wie ungezählte Schüsse.
Das Gesicht ist ein Geruch.
Ein unbekannter Ort.
Ein letzter Blick auf Fuentevaqueros.

Der Geruch ist ein zerstörtes Grab.
Erde.

Ears of the fringes.
To fray the sounds.
Like a Sicilian song.
A country wedding.
Silesia after the Walk.
A migratory bird.
To Bohemia.
To Patagonia.

So, the foreign has her scent.
Streets of houses.
Buenos Aires everywhere.
Buenos Aires tangling on a string.
The songs.
Melancholia.
Her as fool.
As translator.
Across the face.
An escaping bandoleon.[106]
The death outside.
These fingers.
These cold fingers.
Afterwards.

Despierto.
La despierto.
So, the night has a face.
Her face,
a scent.
The face is an ambush
like uncounted shots.
The face is a scent.
An unknown place.
A last glimpse on Fuentevaqueros.

The scent is a destroyed grave.
Earth.

Augeworfenes Meer.
Der Geruch ist immer ein Meer.
Nerudas Matrosen.
Liebe.
Veräußertes Ertrinken.
Geworbene Liebe,
die in Albertis Meer nach Atem ringt.
Der Geruch ist ihr Morgen.
Ihr Aufwachen.
Eingewoben.
Ein Morgen,
der sich verirrt,
aus dem Fenster streift.
Ein Roman.
Ausgebreitet.
Ein Ozean.
Ein Stück Holz,
das der Küste zutreibt.
Immer zutreibt.
Ein Geruch,
der sich bewirtet.
Begastet.
Ufert.
Einfremdet.
Fault.
Der Geruch ist ein Stück Holz.
Übriggeblieben.
Eingebrannte Spuren.
Begangene Fährten,
in denen ich aufwache.
Jahresringe aus Ruß.

Ich wache auf.
Despierto.
En la madrugada de la noche.
Su olor.
In wechselbaren Städten.

Banked up ocean.
The scent is always an ocean.
Neruda's[107] sailors.
Love.
Melted into drowning.
Courted love
that catches her breath in Alberti's[108] ocean.
The scent is her morning.
Her waking up.
Interwoven.
A morning
that is going astray,
streaking out of the window.
A novel.
Spread out.
An ocean.
A piece of wood
floating toward the shore.
Ever floating.
A scent
hosting itself.
Guesting.
Coasting.
For orienting.
Rotting.
The scent is a piece of wood.
Left over.
Burned-in traces.
Inspected tracks
in which I wake up.
Year rings out of soot.

I wake up.
Despierto.
En la madrugada de la noche.
Su olor.
In interchangeable cities.

Gassen wie Gesichter.
Gerüche der Feuer.
Feuerrauch in Städten.
Landschaften der Fremde,
die vererbt werden.
Brache.
Mutierter Geruch schließlich,
eingeschlichen.

Feuergeschmack auf den Zungen.
Der Geruch ist ein Feuer,
das man gelegt hat.
Immer legt.
Selbstbewacht.
Bloße Worte.
Feuer.
Das betrunkene Gelächter der Brandstifter.
Das betrunkene Gelächter der Gerechten,
der Immergerechten,
die nach Wasser fahnden.
Nicht finden.
Zündeln.
Der Geruch ist das kalte Auflauern der Suchenden.
Dieser Geruch.
Hämende Suche.
Dies gläserne Aufwachen der Atemzüge.
Zersprungen.
Feuergeworden.
Geruch der Ackerfurchen ins Meer.
Olor de muerte.
Siempre muerte.
Erde zu löschen.
Feuer zu legen.
Fuego ins Du.
Ins Du der Brand.
Gerodetes Du.
Der Andere.

Alleyways, faces simultaneously.
Scents of the fires.
Fire smoke in the cities.
Landscapes of being foreign,
inherited.
Fallow land.
Mutated scent after all,
crept in.

Taste of fire on the tongues.
The scent is a fire
that was set.
Is always set.
Self-watched.
Sheer words.
Fire.
The drunken laughter of the arsonists.
The drunken laughter of the righteous,
the everrighteous
in hot pursuit of water.
Do not find it.
Fanning the flames.
The scent is the cold trap of searchers.
This scent.
A malice search.
This glassy awakening of breaths.
Broken into pieces.
Turned to a fire.
Scent of furrows into the ocean.
Olor de muerte.
Siempre muerte.
To extinguish earth.
To set on fire.
Fuego into You.
Into You the blaze.
Cutover You.
The Other.

Despierto.
La despierto.
Siempre despertaré.
Immer.

A Ricardo Bada,
al andaluz de Huelva

Despierto.
La despierto.
Siempre despertaré.
Ever.

A Ricardo Bada,[109]
al andaluz de Huelva

buchstabe T

kristall nach T
greift/ wie
konsonanten fällen gläsern
zerspringen
in den sauberen gasthöfen

mir den ekel dieses hasses abwischen
mit dem lappen erinnerung
nicht die taten-/ und
dieses wortgemetzel
dieses schlachtfest sprache
danach

ich frage euch
wohin damit?
wohin?

jetzt
da die mülltonnen überspecken
bleibt vorzeit
die hirnzurücks
wieder startschüsse
renovember

wie ein unfall
dieses T im alphabet

letter T

crystal nigh T[110]
grabs/ as
consonants fell glassy
shatter
in the clean taverns

wipe this disgust off me
with the cloth remembrance
not the atrocities-/ and
this word massacre
and this slaughter fest language
afterwards

I ask you
what to do with it?
what?

now
when the dustbins are overfed
remains foretime
that brainbackwards
again starting shots
renovember

like an accident
this T in the alphabet

neunter november

wie die nebel nachtmahlen
in der morgendämmerung schon

wie herbstblätter farben mahnen
die erde erinnerung kaut

wie die gräber versteinern
die wortlappen der trauernden

wie selbst die leisetreter stocken
wenn die toten offenliegen

wie ich diesen versen mißtraue
über fragen wünschelruten

wie ich sieche antworten belehne
sie zwischen bücher kehre

wie die leben ehrfürchten
die augensklaven bleichen

wie der wind doch nicht fasten will
gedichte in die landschaft kritzelt

zehnter november

ninth of november[111]

how fogs etch off the night
at the break of dawn so soon

how fall leaves urge the color
and earth chews up memories

how the graves change to stone
the wordcloths of the mourners

how even creepers stumble
when the dead lie uncovered

how I distrust these verses
over questions divining rods

how I am ailing weighting answers
sweep them in between books

how the lives are awe-stricken
the eyecaptives deathly pale

how at last the wind refuses to fast
and scrawls poems into the land

tenth of november

anatomie der zeit

gegen
den raum
nimmt die mondin
ab
die sonne/ der sonne
brennt das glashaus ein

niedergeworfen
treibt die wöchnerin
bauchlings rachen

so kalt
so kalt

die geburt

die stundenzeiger kommen
zu verstand

die uhr atmet aus

anatomy of time

toward
the room
wanes
the moones
s
the sun, (s)he
burns-/in the glass house

thrown down in puerperal
weeks she presses her revenges
in prone

so cold
so cold

BIRTH

short hands coming
to their senses

the hour exhales

buchstabe S

Solingens messer sind rot
sorot/ diesrot
beschliffen

känguruhsprung gepeitscht
dies siegfriedstemmen
die masse
historienbeutel vorwärtsruck
kopfzerwalzt

Solingens messer sind deutsch
gedörfelt/ gestädtet
zu meucheln

dies dunkelste der augen
behaust
buchstabe S
legt klagefeuer/ dein damalsruf
gelbstern
trampelt den tag zuniederst
erbeugtes säumt die nacht
zusammengeflicktes lachen
speit das künftige
in den stuben der republik
wird gegen die trauer ermittelt

Solingens särge sind rot
mondbesichelte heimkehr
türkisch
nicht nur

Solingens särge sind deutsch
auch/ besonders/ und

letter S

Solingen's[112] knives are red
sored/ thisred
sharpened

kanguruhop whipped
such siegfriedakimbo11314
the masses
chroniclepouch sudden swing forward
tossed/ turned in head

Solingen's knives are german
by vill/ages/ by ci/ties
to assas/sin/ate

this darkest of the eyes
inha/bite/d
letter S
sets a lamentblaze/ your backthencry
yellowstar
stamps the day far down
something bent bordering the night
pieced up laughter
spits the forthcoming
in the nation's snuggeries
mourning is indicted

Solingen's coffins are red
crescent-shape/d homecoming
turkish
not only

Solingen's coffins are german
as well/ especially/ and

zeit in der sich die blicke ändern

es hatte zu brennen aufgehört
versehrt kehrte die stille heim
ein verbündeter im november
war ihr mein zuhause

die buchstaben sollten sich paaren
zu unwägbaren licht

zungengeläufiger taumel
mit jedem wort aus wasser
so aufgedunsen war die furcht
zu bleiben

time when glances change

it had ceased to burn
silence returned home hurt
an ally in november
was my home to her

letters were to pair
to imponderable light

tonguecurrent reeling
with every word made of water
that's how bloated the fear was
to stay

Austernfischer, Marinero, Vogelfrau
1997

Oysterfisher, Marinero, Womanbird

vogelfrau III

flügelwort zur meerin
ruderlaut der luft

vom saum der sprache
in wortes stille

womanbird III

wingword to the oceaness
rowingsound of air

from the seam of language
in word's silence

du sprichst

selten mit deinem mund/ mundschweigen so
stillmeerig sanftwellen (fast ruhe oder
zartgeworden) dumund ichmund einmund dein
wort aus augenweiten augenlippen berührung
ein wimpernschlag duschweigen
wie anschmiegsame stille, marinero, fast schon
dämmerung oder rosenhimmel dein gang die
pirouetten aus mundwinkeln: wehung

und tanzt begehren (ich will dich) jetzt
morgen gestern
über den rand der gläser tassen melodie so
klangvoll nichtwortrund so kreisend ab-
wandernd brisenflaum wie zerbrechliches
luftstocken mit beiden händen am nebelhorn

you speak

seldom with your mouth/ mouthsilence so
calmstream mellowwaves (almost quiet or
becoming gentle) youmouth mymouth amouth your
word from eyewideness eyelips smooth touches
a blink a wink youwithoutword
as sinuous silence, marinero, almost
dawning even rosy heaven your motion the
pirouettes out of mouthmoments: storming

and dancing desire (I want you) now
tomorrow yestermorning
over the edge of the glasses mugs melody so
tuneful nonwordround so circling down
wandering breezy hair like fragile
air taken away with both hands at the misthorn

„Denke daran, daß ich auch Rose bin" (Rafael Alberti)

1
blüht die weiße
rose mein laken

öffnet das weiße
laken mein fenster

kehrt das weiße
fenster zur nacht

empfängt die weiße
nacht mir luna

wie kaltes fieber
der mond danach

2
dies nüchterne blau
die schweigende hand

ergießt sich stille
das lippenpaar

3
die mondin war
scheues olivengesicht
seidener hain
dein haar

4
blaue rose
matrosin der nacht
die mondin streut falten
mond dem schoß

"Keep in mind, I am also a rose" (Rafael Alberti)

1
blooms the white
rose my linen

opens the white
linen my window

turns the white
window to night

receives the white
night luna for me

like cold fever
later the moon

2
this bald blue
the silent hand

calmness pours itself
the pair of lips

3
the mooness was
oliveface shy
silken grove
your hair

4
blue rose
night's sailorette
the mooness strews lines
a moon to the lap

ich erde ein
den geruch

5
so kämmen wir lippen
die münder fort
erneut die hände
haarpfade lang
unsere schieren körper bloß
bewelken die mondin die rose

I earth in
the scent

5
so we comb lips
the mouths away
once again the hands
along hair trails
our sheer bodies bare
we wither the mooness the rose

„VOM blau,
das noch sein Auge sucht,
trink ich als erster"
Paul Celan

tag einundzwanzig, retina der Märzin

taucht gegend um milchglas kristallene lider
ins raunen vor morgigem tauwurf der zeit
mit stotternden fingern zum flußlauf der hand
ich taste mich heim die firnstrecken fort

ein reißsaum der sägblätter rostpfade älter
berindet den fransenden abschied der nacht
geschulterte tage entzingeltes eis
erlog uns die schminke des winters den raum

aus luftzweigen zittert ein stimmbares echo
in porende wälder zaust ädriger hall
die pflugspur der vögel schart augendes blau
vor grüner tonsur faltet stirnfurchen frei

pulst leise die sonne verletzbare verse
dem flüsternden flaumspiel der farben anheim
den lauten des sanges der brache erweckt
beatmen die lippen den nacken um frost

"FROM the blue,
still searching its eye,
I will drink as first one"
Paul Celan

day twentyone, the Marchess' retina

steeps scenery round tinted glass crystalline eyelids
into whisper before tomorow's thawthrow of time
with stammering fingers to the hand's river course
feeling my way home follow firn journeys along

a severing seam of saw blades rustingpaths older
lignifies the fringing farewell of this other night
shouldered daybreaks daytimes decircled ice
winter's make up made up a wintery space for us

from skybranches shivers a tunable echo
into stomata woods whooshes veiny resonance
birds' p:low flight leaves traces and scratches eyeing blue
before a green tonsure and frees the furrowing brow

the sun pulses softly vulnerable verses
ever entrusted to the color's cottony play
awakened for the fallow ground's song and its tune
see lips breathe in and into the neck to rescue the freeze

fernlautmetz
2000

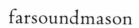

farsoundmason

fremdw:ort

das so leicht nicht sag-
bar ist und wird

aus den angeln
gehobene nähe

foreign wor(l)d

that is not easily say-
able and will (not) be

closeness
lifted off its hinges

augustvoll mond

augnacht wacht am wind
im windohr
schlürft oboenferne aus-

wärts auch ich
sing mit
im astohr mund und klang

vom versrand her
mondgesät und lippensacht
lakensaum der luft

auch ich sing mit
die augnacht weit
ganz baum und todesleicht

augustful moon

eyenight keeping sight at the wind
in the windear
slurping oboe shores out-

side as I am
singing along
in the boughear mouth and sound

from the verse fringe
moonseeded mellowlipped
sheetseam of the air

and I sing too along
my eyenight far
be all tree and deathlike feathery

andalusische treppe für T.

„zum licht gehen — Andalucía, Anda-
Lucía" sagte vater : wie SCHWEIGEN
in lichtbringerin/ wie in einleuchtend
die eigene ethymologie weitersteigern/
steigern nach unten
sagte vater „nacht,
ins schwarz-
licht vergossenes dunkelöl"

er schrieb ins familienbuch
„stammbaum, unbekannt gefällt. 1936
zweijährig/ 1939 FÜNF"
er schrieb auf die
lebenslinie:
                oliven-
                luft
                        gewitter-
                        blau
                                nacht-
                                herkunft

„lost generation"[114] sagte er nie

andalusian stairs for T.

"going to the light — Andalucía, Anda-
Lucía" said father : as SILENCE
in she-who-brings-the-light/ as in enlightening
further raising your own etymology/
raising downwards
said father "night,
dark-
oil spilled into black light"

he wrote into the family book
"family tree, felled unknown. 1936
two years old/ 1939 FIVE"
he wrote onto the
lifeline:
        olive-
        air
            tempest-
            blue
                    night-
                    origin

he never said "generación perdida"

Berlin, an-
gezählte stadt
        (next round) hör

nach dem kaiser-
schnitt das mauerfleisch
in hinterhöfen stöhnen auf
reißbrettfiebersiegessäulen
embryonenschwämme, usw.
(WECKGLASNOSTALGIE)

pilzen lautstumm aus archiven
metastasen butterblumen
—Döblins mordung—
zugedeckt und renoviert
„die traurigen Geranien"
gebierst du augen-
greisin mut-
ter: straßen-
mädchen, junge kunft die not
auf die eingelegten dörfer
welt um nabel: menschen

die aus zerbombten plätzen
nachgefahren trockentränken
zuchtgesichter, viehbereite
in sterilen chromgehöften

Berlin, count-
ed down city
        (next round) hear

after the kaiserian-
section wallflesh
in the courtyards groaning on
drawingtablefevervictorycolumns
embryorot, etc.
(JARGLASSNOSTALGIA)

mushrooming from archives death-muted
metastases buttercups
—Döblin's[115] murdering—
covered and renovated
"the Melancholy Geraniums"[116]
you birth giving eyes-
aged woman mother
courage: street-
walker, young in labor and woe
on the pickled villages
world surrounding navel: people

who from bombed squares
descended dry drinking throughs
breed faces readily brute
in sterile chrome BACKcourts

subversives mosaik Unter den Linden
(ein sprechstück für acht männerstimmen)

I
jedes ungeborene wort
gräbt furchen in deine stirn
faltet gedanken wie maulwürfe
boden auf/ unter den füßen
hügeln – ich erwarte erdig sprache

jedes gesprochene wort
näht flügel zusammen
nachgedacht ein ort
nah der küste mensch

jedes morgige wort
wie zweifelsfälle verse
ist mein gedicht
ein koffer in der hand
dir entgegenzufliehen

II
jedes ungeborene wort
in deine stirn gräbt furchen
faltet wie maulwürfe gedanken-
boden auf/ unter den füßen
hügeln – ich erwarte
erdig sprache

jedes undgesprochene wort
zusammen näht flügel
nachgedacht ein ort
nah der küste mensch

jedes morgende wort
wie zweifelsfälle verse
der gestrigdeutschen silben
end/heil/rampen/mahl-

146

subversive mosaic Unter den Linden[117]
(a non-play play for eight male voices)

I
every unborn word
digs furrows into your forehead
folding thoughts like moles[118]
raise ground/ beneath the feet
hills — earthy I await language

every spoken word
sews wings together
pondered a place
seeming the coast named human

every tomorrow's word
like cases of doubt verses
is my poem
a suitcase in the hand
fleeing into you

II
every unborn word
in your forehead digs furrows
folding like moles raise thought-
ground/ beneath the feet
hills — I await
language earthy

every andspoken word
together sews wings
pondered a place
seeming the coast named human

every morrowing word
like cases of doubt verses
the die-hard german syllables
end/heil/rampen/mahl-

zeit ist mein gedicht
ein koffer in der hand
dir zu/ entgegenfliehen

III
jedes ungeborene wort
in deine stirn gräbt furchen
faltet wie maulwürfe gedanken-
boden auf/ unter den füßen
hügeln – ich erwarte
Unter den Linden/ erdig
sprache aschen

jedes undgesprochene wort
zusammen näht flügel nach-
gedacht ein ort
naht der küste mensch/ nah
die küste mensch

jedes morgende wort
die zweifelsfälle verse
der gestrigdeutschen silben
endheil/ rampen/ mahl-
zeit ist mein gedicht
ein koffer der hand
dir zu/ entgegen/ fliehen

IV
jedes angeborene wort
in deiner stirn grab/ furcht-
falt die maulwürfe, gedanken-
boden, auf unter den füßen
hügeln – ich er warte!
Unter den Linden büßen
erdensprachig aschen

zeit[119] is my poem
a suitcase in the hand
into you/ fleeing again

III
every unborn word
into your forehead digs furrows
folding like moles raise thought-
ground/ under the feet
hills – I await
Unter den Linden/ earthy
language ashen

every andspoken word
together sews wings a pond
ered place
seam of the coast named human/ seeming
the coast's name

every morning word
the cases of doubt verses
the die-hard german syllables
endheil/rampen/mahl-
zeit is my poem
a suitcase for the hand
into you/ against/ fleeing

IV
every inborn word
in your forehead burrow/ rows of fear
manifolding the moles, thought
ground, on under the feet
hills – I he wait!
Unter den Linden pleading
earthen-lingual ashes

jedes undgesprochene wort
zusammen näht flügel nach
gedacht ein ort:
saat der küste mensch/ naht
die klippe mensch
Oranienburgerstraße

jedes morgende wort/ fort
die zweifelsfälle verse
die gestrigdeutschen silben
endheilrampenmahl-
zeit ist mein gedicht
ein hoffen der hand
dir zugegenfliehen

V
jedes eingeborene wort
in deiner stirn grab
furchtfalt der maulwürfe, gedankenboden
aufmarsch unter den füßen
hügel – ich er sie tecum!
Unter den Linden büßen
erdensprachig aschen

jedes undgesprochene wort
zusammen – näht flügel nach
gedacht ein ort:
saat der küste mensch/ naht
die klippe mensch
Oranienburgerstraße

jedes morgende wort/ fort
die zweifelsfälle verse
die gestrigdeutschen silben:
endheilrampenmahlzeit
ist mein gedicht

every andspoken word
together double-sewed wings a
pondered place:
seed of the coast named human/ seamingly
the cliff of man
Oranienburgerstraße[120]

every morning word/ gone
the cases of doubt verses
the die-hard german syllables
endheilrampenmahl-
zeit is my poem
to h/open the hand
fleeing withinyou

V
every native-born word
in your forehead burrow
fearfold of the moles, thoughtground
marching on under the feet
hill – I he she tecum!
Unter den Linden pleading
earthen-lingual ashes

every andspoken word
together – double sews wings
pondering a place:
seed of the coast named human/ seamingly
the cliff of man
Oranienburgerstraße

every morning word/ gone
the cases of doubt verses
the die-hard german syllables
endheilrampenmahlzeit
is my poem

ein hoffen hand
dir zugegen du

VI
jedes angebürtige wort
auf deiner stirn ein grab
furchtfalt der maulwürfe
gedankenboden
maul-wurf auf-marsch
unterfüßig den füßen
hügeln – er sie tecum ich:
Unter den Linden: Grüßen!
Hordensprache Asche Heil!

jedes undgesprochene wort
zusammen näht flügel nach
gedächtnisort
saat der küste mensch
ist die klippe mensch
Oranienburgerstraße

jedes morgende wort/ fort
die zweifelsfällerverse
die gestrigdeutschen silben:
endheilrampenmahlzeit

mein gedicht ist
einhoffen hand
dir zugegen ich
ein du

VII
jedes angebürtige wort
auf deiner stirn ein grab:
furchtfalt der maulwürfe

a hope/n hand
to you within you

VI
every native-born word
on you forehead a barrow
fearfold of the moles
thoughtground
moles whack on-marching
subfoot the feet
hills — he she tecum I:
Unter den Linden: Salute!
Hordelanguage Ashes Heil!

every andspoken word
together double sews wings
a wondering place
seed of the coast named human
is the cliff of man
Oranienburgerstraße

every morning word/ gone
the doubtfell case verses
the die-hard german syllables:
endheilrampenmahlzeit

my poem is
ahope/n hand
to you within myself
a you

VII
every native-born word
on your forehead a barrow:
fearfold of the moles

gedankenboden
maul-wurf auf-marsch
unterfüßig den füßen
hügeln – er sie tecum ich:
Unter den Linden: Grüßen!
Hordensprechchor: Asche Heil!

jedes ungebrochene wort
zusammen/ näht flügel nach:
gedächtnisort –
saat der küste mensch
ist die klippe mensch, memento!
Oranienburgerstraße

jedes morgende wort/ fort
die zweifelsfällerverse
die gestrigdeutschen silben
endheilmahlzeitrampen

mein gedicht ist
einhoffende hand
die zugegen ich
ein du ein ich

VIII
jedes angebürtige wort
auf deiner stirn ein grab:
furchtfalt der maulwürfe
gedankenboden
maul-wurf auf-marsch
unterfüßig zu füßen den füßen
hügeln Er Sie tecum Ich:
Unter den Linden: Grüßen!
Hordensprechchor: Asche Heil!

thoughtground
moles whack on-marching
subfoot the feet
hills — he she tecum I:
Unter den Linden: Salute!
Hordelanguage chorus: Ashes Heil!

every unbroken word
together/ double sews wings:
a wondering place about —
seed of the coast named human
is the cliff of man, memento!
Oranienburgerstraße

every morning word/ gone
the doubtfell case verses
the die-hard german syllables:
endheilmahlzeitrampen

my poem is
an opend hand
to you within myself
a you a me

VIII
every native-born word
on your forehead a barrow:
fearfold of the moles
thoughtground
moles whack on-marching
subfoot underfoot the feet
hills He She tecum I:
Unter den Linden: Salute!
Hordelanguage chorus: Ashes Heil!

jedes ungesprochene wort
zusammen/ mäht flügelnacht
gedächtnis fort: falsches schweigen:
saat der küste mensch. Memento!
Oranienburgerstraße

jedes morgende wort/ fort
die zweifelsfällerverse
die gestrigdeutschen silben:
endheilmahlzeitrampen

mein gedicht ist wort
hoffen die hand
die zugegen ich
ein du ein ich
mein gedicht mein wort

every unspoken word
together/ wings mown down unseen
a wander-about place: the wrong silence:
seed of the coast named human. Memento!
Oranienburgerstraße

every mourning word/ gone
the doubtfell case verses
the die-hard german syllables:
endheilmahlzeitrampen

my poem is word
hope/n the hand
that within myself
a you a me
my poem my word

Tentoonstelling II

auf dem weg nach Purmerend
standen die wächsernen birken
gleich ketzerinnen vor gericht
vergelbten an bushaltestellen
zu knöchrigen büßergestalten

jinete, jinete, la muerte

aus rupfenden kolkschwarzen augen
verstarrten beschnittene stämme
die mähne der gäule
begreisten den sturm
im altkalten abschritt oktobergalopp

jinete, jinete, la muerte

die graugreisen strähnen des regens
im schädel die lautlosen zügel
verschlierten den blick
die qualmenden häuser
beräucherten menschengerippe

jinete, jinete, la muerte

die birken sie trugen die kronen
aus elenden knochen zur scham
und fledderten windtriebig blätter
den dichtern fürs wortene aas
die grachten zerbrachen das zwielicht

jinete, jinete, la muerte
la vida es son de la muerte

Tentoonstelling II

on the way to Purmerend
were waxen birches standing
like female heretics before court
awaiting a bus they withered
into lanky penitent figures

jinete, jinete, la muerte

from plucking crowblack eyes
scowled the trimmed trunks stiff
the manes of the nags
travellaged the tempest
in oldcold gait octobergallop

jinete, jinete, la muerte

the greyaged hair of rain
in the skull the soundless reins
veiled the vision
the smoldering houses
smoked men's women's skeletons

jinete, jinete, la muerte

the birches they carried the crowns
out of woebegone bones for shame
and robbed stormsprouted leaves
for the poets their lingual carrion
but dutch canals tore the twilight apart

jinete, jinete, la muerte
la vida es son de la muerte

Bogotá I

der himmel keucht sich stadt-
geschichten/ verzittert
splittersilhouetten/ franst aus
gedankenstriche punktstumm Punkt.
Semikolon; frage mensch? aus-
rufe zieren efeugrün den
ziegelroten jung-fern-mantel
eigentlich [man:tél] ein überwurf
der freiluft wölbt/ vermißt/ nimmt maß
ein geschirmtes blau, kein komma
in der Hoffnungsstraße, sprich:
Esperanza (atemkomma), sie
abgefreit und weißbehelmt
notier: akupunktiert/ pariert
ein MG-Soldat –
dem eisenlauf als fingerpfand
und augskalpell der stadt

sein gesicht ist jung/ geschultert

Bogotá I

the sky wheezes city-
stories for himself/ jitters
shiversilhouettes/ fray s
re marks soft dot Full Stop.
Semicolon; question human? being ex
clamations decorating ivygreen the
brick-red Virgin-Mairy-mantle
meaning [man:tél] a s
leeve arching breezy freedom/ misses/ aim ing
a screened blue, no comma
in South Hope Street, say:
Esperanza (a breathcomma), them,
unfreed and white helmeted
punctuate: acupunctured/ commanded
a MG-soldier –
a fingerpledge to the iron barrel
and the city's eyescalpel

his face is young/ shouldered

die straßenschuhe von Nachig

sind ein geschenktes gehsteigpflaster/ die
nackten füße dreck-
gehauen: ein rückenbündel holz
führt jeder frau
den weg zurück in körperbeugen

auf der erde hockt geschichte
spannt unbestellte stille
das fingeralphabet der alten

mein schweigen kostet einen dollar
und jeder schnappschuss wort/bild klang
ist unversöhnter handel/

auch dies gedicht

the street shoes of Nachig

are a paving given as present/ the
bare feet dirt-
beaten: a backbundle wood
leads for every woman
the way back into bowed down bodies

on the ground squats history
spans unworked stillness
the fingerspelling of the elders

my silence costs a dollar
and every snapshot word/image sound
is a trade unreconciled/

as this poem

Zona Rosa, farbort-

fliesen menschenflimmer
ins lichtermix gekämmt, wie
man bilder kämmt dem auge

ein bettler (am stock)
[amulett >>muleta<<], die
abhustende alte, greises
gründelweib der häusersockel
GottSegneSie – 5
pesos kostet der satz

lebenspärchen stricher nutten
allenthalben uniformen
und hand-aufs-herz, schrägnational/
sirenen cafés ambulantes

ein mädchen springt mit traurigblick
kaut im augmund brot, die
hand ist weltauf hingestreckt
dem dollargringo

Zona Rosa, colorplace-

tiles peopleflickering
combed into the mix of lights, like
images are combed to the eye

a beggar (with cane)
[amulet >>muleta<<], the
coughing up crone, aged
dabble dame of plinth walls
GodBlessYou – 5
pesos for this sentence

l:overs hustlers hookers
everywhere uniforms
and hand-at-heart, slash national/
sirens cafés ambulatory

a girl hops with doleful mien
chewing in her eyemouth bread, the
hand thrusted out wi:de openly
to the dollargringo

nachtrandspuren
2002

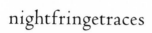

nightfringetraces

kompaß & dämmerung

Da ist der osten weit hinter meiner stirn. Da
ist der westen ein pfandaug *hei*
matt. Da ist der süden würfel
becher dem hunger. Da ist der NORDEN. *No*
pierdas el norte. Da ist ostwest
laibung der sonne. Da ist der mond
auf seiner suche nach dem zwiegeschlecht. Da ist
die SPRACHZEITLOSE licht
verzweigung der vogelunruh. Da ist tau
brotwärme im verlegten w:ort
ist stille noch. Da ist der tag
so reichbar nah

compass & twilight

There is the east far behind my brow. There
is the west a pawn gaze *homelan(d)*
guid. There is the south dice
box for the hunger. There is the NORTH. *No*
pierdas el norte. There is eastwest
loafing of the sun. There is the moon
on his search for the twi-gender. There is
SPEECH TIME LESS light
branching of the birds disquiet. There is dew
bread-warmth in the displaced wor(l)d
is silence still. There is the day
so reachable close

abschied und schwer-

fallen/ das von den lippen fällt
schwer und zu sagende *ich hab/*
ich hab dich und sagte
mir ein hörgast sie benutzen so
worte so w:orte wie frage ich
zurück wie liebe und sehn

:sucht

aber dies sprachschwere nach
:schwere gefälle am eingekerbten
blick aber diese abschiede und
die lippen wie ausgespannt fern
:offen unter der fragiler w:erdenden
worthaut die bricht mit jeder
berührung nach
platzt aber die plötzlichkeit der
haut das brüchige wort das sich
behauptet still und kopfstreichelt
aber die weißhaarigen bilder der
abschied nah *me* abschiedsMUT

TER wie sich ihr schloh
weißgott ihr leib blut
und wasser wie sie nichts
mehr sagt und

farewell and heavy-

falling/ that falls off the lips
heavy having to say *I have*/
I have you and a listening guest
told me you use such
words such wor(l)ds as I ask
in return as love and wish

:fullness

but this language weight after
:weight decline at the engrailed
gaze but these farewells and
lips like stretched out afar
:open beneath the word skin
be(com)ing more fragile
which brakes with
any touch after
bursts however the suddenness
of skin the brashly word that
strikes still head-strokes
but the snow haired pictures the
farewell n(e)a(r) *me* farewellCOURAGE

MOTHER how her snow colored
heaven knows her body blood
and water when she does not
speak anymore and

mutter & sprache

herzuhr sagst du *die herzuhr*
geht langsamer. Wir

konnten die zeit
nicht mehr einholen. Es war

kein sprechen mehr kein
ankommen. Nur

diese stille die uns die augen
wog. Du

hattest mir den mund gegeben
die hände die uns erzählten. Ich

kehre wort um wort zurück
und vertraue dem ende.

mother & tongue

hearthour you say *the hearthour*
runs slower. We

could not recover
time anymore. There was

no speaking anymore no
arrival. Only

this stillness that weighed
our eyes. You

had given me the mouth
the hands that spoke to us. I

return word for word
and trust in the end.

novemberaug des raben

cuervo krähe crow, drei-
w:ort dämmerschmelze/ seidensieb (ein blau
verglänzen) am frühen nachmittag. Im tal
hängt dunkel matt vom tiefgewölk &
schliert wie augen die übernächtigt
sich selbst in ihre ränder stürzen. In schwarzer flechte
     schleift
verhören den kalender
faßt herbst und treibt auf sturz des helleren
wie mooslichtdunst sich saugt ans tannennetz/ ein
     erdkreuzstich
ins blinde. Ein fleckenriß
ein scherbenschrei die folgen
der starre rufer stiert gekrächz
das seinen blick sich beutet
dem vogel ausgeliefert

novembereye of the raven

cuervo krähe crow, three-
wor(l)d twilightmelt/ silkensieve (one blue
deglow) in the early afternoon. In the valley
lingers darkness dimmed from clouds laying low &
blurred like eyes that blearily
throw themselves into their brinks. In black lichen
        over
hearing drags the calendar
grabs the fall driving for a tumble of the brighter
as mossmistlight draws toward the mesh of fir/ a
        dirt cross stitch
into the blind. A patch torn through
a shardcry the answer
the stiff caller stares a caw
that preys upon her own gaze
at the mercy of the bird

salto mortale

haftet die zunge am wort
das wort an der zunge
die stadt haftet die stadt
am aug dirigiert das ohr
schnecken.symphonisch
die hand die hand noch die
gespreizten finger zunge
rückwärts aug vorwärts
das wort haftet das wort

salto mortale

tongue clings to the word
word to the tongue
the city clings the city
on the eye the ear conducts
snail.symphonic
the hand the hand still the
stilted fingers tongue
backwards eye forwards
the word clings the word

Sydney-Canberra

denk dir zug und gleis springer
oder bahn schlitten fahrt post
kutschen geholper (in memoriam)
ohne überfall dafür zitter kritzel
die worte rauben die buchstaben
kaum zu entziffern auf dem papier
danach in der ferne schafe
zwischen verendetem holz. Denk dir baum
aas und fahles eukalyptusweiß
beinhauslandschaften jahre
nach dem gemetzel. Klar wie die lupennähe
küftiger gräber. Im bild noch
eine herde augen. Denk sie dir
känguruhscheu.

Sydney-Canberra

imagine train and tracks hopper
or railway sledge ride stage
coaches bumping (in memoriam)
no inroad but jitter scribble
words robbing letters
barely to decipher on paper
later in distance sheep
in between perished wood. Imagine tree carri-
on and pale eucalyptus white
mortuarylandscapes years
after the carnage. Clear as the magnified closeness
of future graves. In the image still
a herd of eyes. Imagine them
kangaroo shy.

martinete

amboß uhrpuls ahnen
laut schlag eisen
hammer eine stimme mono

ton metalle splittern glut die nach
kunft gleißt sich vorzurück
ins moll gegossen vom

stoß gesang im amboß schlag
im mund kristall
erspannte zeit die gerbt

geschichtenhaut (altvordertakt)
die lippen *pilgern* sich entlang
behaust sind hinter gitterstäben

im fort und her gebeugten tag der folgt
den längst verlassenen höhlen
die schatten die sich lieder schmieden

martinete

anvil timepulse traces
thunk hit iron
hammer a voice mono

tone metal splitting blaze the after
hereafter glistens itself backwardforth
casted into A minor by

stroke of song an anvil blow
in mouth crystal
tautened hour that tans

his storiesskin (for forebear beat)
the lips *pilger* themselves along
rehoused and behind bars

in a seesaw crooked day that follows
the long forsaken caves
shadows forging songs each other

dichter ort II

im hautgrund die uhr
ins nirgendwo der zeit
als das auge noch meer war

a poet's pace II

on skinground the hour
into the void of time
when still the eye was sea

die tür

die tür in den händen die
das fenster verschloss das
fenster am boden die
tür der glassplitt unter den
füßen der boden
spiegelt das fenster die
tür das fenster durch die
wir die tür das
fenster uns schließen. Kein
wort. Uns entkommen.

the door

the door in our hands that
closed the window the
window on the ground
the door the glass splint beneath our
feet the ground
mirrors the window the
door the window through which
we close the door the
window for us. No
word. We escaped ourselves.

Altpieschen. Bäume 2

vereinzelt fassaden entwerfen schriften
FINDELSCHRIFTEN nach dem regen. Wände
die mich lesen. Den ziegelstein das mauer
werk besprechen hergeputzte mörtelnarben. Über
die abwesenheit der ulme schweigen
spitzhorn und buche im rindenalphabet
sind wir uns einig, *nomadensüchtig*

Altpieschen. Trees 2

here & there facades composing scripts
FOUNDLINGSCRIPTS after the rain. Walls
that are reading me. Over-plastered mortar
scars bespeak the brick stone the stonework. About
the absence of the elm remain silent
road-leafed tree and birch in the bark alphabet
we are at one with eachother, *nomad-addicted*

14. Juli. Bürger-

straße. Auf der giebelspitze gegenüber
landet unverhofft eine elster. Sie putzt sich
wie eine katze. Ich schreibe

diesen satz auf die straße
blicke hoch und beide sind fort. So
stelle ich mir GESCHICHTE vor.

14th of July. Bürger-

straße.[121] On the gable peak vis-à-vis
lands unexpectedly a magpie. She grooms
herself like a cat. I write

this sentence onto the street
look up and both are gone. This
is how I imagine HISTORY.

„*Du, Erinnerung, halte fest, wie sie waren.*"
(Konstantinos Kavafis)

Alexandria, verinnert

den epilog vorüberheiten
im dichten ort. Die augen

saphirblau, ganz meerin. Eros
gegenwart: Kavafis

im aufgedeckten bett
die zerriebene geographie

der straßen. Er
traute sich die stille zu

die den baren versen folgt
und der versehrten lust. Dann

nahm er die frühen spiegel
von den worten und entwarf

die zeit. Licht-
opal, nachtjasmin

nachmittags. Im zimmer
die stadt vor seinem fenster

wie unbeirrt. Am rande
des begreifens

ein hautgedächtnis. So
lieh er sich den tod

ins alphabet und schrieb
„Halte fest, Erinnerung!"

und ging wie du

190

Alexandria, reternalized

the epilogue sojourneys
in a poet' s pace. Eyes

sapphireblue, all oceaness. Eros
presence: Kavafis

in the uncovered bed
grated geography

of the streets. He
dared to take the quiet

that follows pure sentences
and wounded delight. Then

he took the ear:ly mirrors
from the words and crafted

time. Light-
opal, nightjasmine

afternoon. At the room
the city outside his window

unflinchingly. On the brink
of sense

a skinmemory. So
he borrowed death

into his alphabet and wrote:
"Hold on, remembrance!"

and left like you

notat für einen brasilianer in München

vom gehör der orte
spricht Ignacio vor dem hybriden
selbstwort des dichters. Immer

wenn er den süden legt
führt sein bleistift den norden
entwirft der kompaß die hand

note for a brazilian in Munich

about the ear of places
speaks Ignacio before the hybrid
self-word of the poet. Always

when he lays the south
his pencil carries the north
creates the compass the hand

finnischer wintervorrat
2005

finnish winter reservoir

abend verglückt mit diesem flammen-
werfer / schattenstreuner [EL SOL] I maskulines

I dürre hälfte buchstabiert
sein weibliches feuer-

pendant [DIE SONNE] lockt
himmelsblätter vor & lichtgeronnen

I lunares heft / sprachluftsaiten
ungebunden. I pastellgüte der farben

: mond & feminin. Irgendwo
I schiffsschraube I weither / monotones ferneisen &

die erzählbaren geschichten / „hör
den vorüberheiten zu" sagte großvater: „dem meer

die lautschrift abringen"
siempre la mar & die kielspur [Machado]

: die kielspur der lautschrift

evening de:lights with this flame-
thrower / shadows estray [EL SOL] I masculine

I barren half spells
his feminine fire-

companion [DIE SONNE] elicits
leaves from on high & lightclotted

I lunar binder / wordwindnotes
unbound. I pastel mallowness of colors

: moon and feminine. Somewhere
I ship propeller I afar / monotone tramping iron &

the tellable stories / "listen
to what past by" said grand-father: "to wrest

the sounds of letters from the sea"
siempre la mar & the fading wake [Machado][123]

: the fading wake of written sounds

wie, 1 erinnerung

wie ich heute nicht mehr weiß
wie der kampf
wie lang die runden
wie er
wie er den namen
wie vater den namen
wie er den namen spanisch
wie er am abend zuvor
wie er den wecker
wie er aufgestanden
wie er mich geweckt
wie ich erwachsen
wie erwachsensein eine uhrzeit
wie erwachsensein ein paar runden
wie afrika ins wohnzimmer
wie mutter noch schlief
wie er sein bier
wie er im unterhemd
wie er mit jedem schlag
wie er kommentierte
wie er mir jeden schlag
wie jeder schlag
wie jeder schlag erwachsensein
wie das bild schwarzweiß
wie er den großen helden
wie wir den großen helden
wie er mein großer held
wie er später zur arbeit
wie er mutter noch
wie er mir duch die haare
wie nachts
wie ich nachts erwachsen
wie jeder schlag
wie jeder schlag erwachsensein
wie Muhammad
wie Muhammad Ali vorwegnahm
wie der kampf ausgeht

how, 1 memory

how I don't know today anymore
how the fight
how   long the rounds
how he
how he   the name
how father   the name
how he   the name spanish
how he   the night before
how he   the alarm
how he got up
how he woke me
how I   grown
how being grown up   a time of night
how being grown up   a few rounds
how africa   into the living room
how mother still slept
how he   his beer
how he   in his undershirt
how he   with every punch
how he commented
how he   every punch to me
how every punch
how every punch   being grown up
how the screen   black and white
how he   the great hero
how we   the great hero
how he   my great hero
how he   later to work
how he still   mother
how he   through my hair
how at night
how I   growing up at night
how every punch
how every punch   being grown up
how Muhammad
how Muhammad Ali gave away
how the fight ends

notat an einem 12. august

sich alles mit leichtigkeit
& vorstellen : sich

die erde
das wasser
die luft

I gehen
I dampfer
den atem. I kommen

den tod

& das feuer
I brandlaib die zungen

I flugzeug
das schwimmen
& gleise im ohr

I verschweifen der laute
traktorenverstöhnen
die heunacht als laken

I Gott

I gebet
I holzkreuz gestrandet

& lichtleichte engel
die schürfwunde der zeit
über die landschaft gefahren I trost

: I schreiben vergessen
im gedicht I begehren
die flügel

& stolpern

note from a 12th of august

anything easily self-imagined
& imagine : Iself

earth
water
air

I leaving
I steamship
breathing. I coming

death

& the fire
I loaf of brand the tongues

I airplane
a swim
& tracks echoing in the head

I disp e(a)r sion of sounds
a tractor groaning away
the haynight as sheet

I God

I prayer
I wooden cross stranded

& light lightangels
the graze of time
driven overland scape I comfort

: I writing forgotten
in the poem I desire
the wings

& stumble

Jyväskylä

SCHNEE

LAND KLANG sich erfinden
& sprechen. Unübersetzt. Ich höre

„Nimm vom Schnee das Ungesagte"

Jyväskylä

SNOW

LAND SOUND inventing yourself
& speaking. Untranslated. I listen

"Take from the snow the unsaid"

4zeiler in Tampere

Kirsikkakakkua. Die Freude
der kinder am kirschkernspucken &
sahnefinger im mund

dem sagen näher

4-liner in Tampere

Kirsikkakakkua. The children's
pleasure of spitting cherry pits &
creamfingers in the mouth

closer to speaking

leinwandengel

Los Angeles. Bilder-

sand auf die
haupt & nebenrollen. Schön-

blut. Mit engelszungen

silverscreen angels

Los Angeles. Picture-

sand onto
leads & supporting roles. Beauti-

ful blood. With tongues of angels

nacht-

glas am Charles River
[lightdropcolumns]
windgeflammt. Hoch
häuser auf zitterpfählen

night-

glass on Charles River
[lichttropfensäulen]
windflamed. High
rises on jitterpilings

nachtblauleicht &

aufgehoben. Unter deinen augen
I hand voll stadt

I mondverleiben. Wir leihen
sein licht in den tag

nightbluelightness &

saved. Under your eyes
I hand full of city

I ful filling moon. We borrow
his light into the day

Boston, februarmorgen

tauben
luft. Vorweggenommen ihr taggestimmtes.
Das kuckucksende
der ampelanlage die zeitvertonung.
Der vorgeschnellte atemstoß
des tages. Die sich schrittergeben
: mülljäger jogger wind
im blechcontainer wird aufbewahrt
I almosenhand / I rauszufischendes
vom zweck am abfallrand

Boston, february morning

pigeon
air. Anticipated their daytune.
Cuckoo end of
the traffic light the timesoundtrack.
Darted out gasp of breath
of the day. The ones measured by steps
: trash hunters joggers wind
in a metal container is kept
I alms hand / I thing one can fish for
from the purpose at the garbage edge

sammler

schuhbändel
offen im plastikbeutel
zum rucksack geschnürt die hände im müll
behälter die flaschen den blick
im plastikbeutel im ruck
sack schlurfend im müll
behälter schuh bändeloffen

: I sohlenpfand der füße

gatherer

shoelaces
untied in a plastic bag
lashed as backpack the hands in the trash
bin the bottles the stare
in the plastic bag on the back
pack shuffling in the garbage
bin shoe laceopen

: I soled refund of the feet

dämmerpalette, figurativ

erd
beerschimmer spiegel
fäden lichtherbstfrühe & reif-
kristall. Ins auberginenglas
kratzt I morgenkritzel sich
aus tintenglanz & ungeschriebenem ans aug
im nachschriftdunkel I mundverlangen heißt I mehr
an atem. „Dies unbesohlte noch des tages". Wind
& kaltsog schreiben. Es streckt die laubenluft [I märz
kämpft an] dem schein nach wärme
auf die körper & farbgesetzte harlekine. Sie
spielen mit dem himmelsschutt dem
graugeröll verträumen sich und ziehen
aus dem ersten licht
I glasversteck

gläserner morgen / I spiegelmorgen

dawning palette, figurative

black
cherryshimmer mirror
threads shining falldaybreak & white frost-
crystal. Into the eggplant jar
scrapes itself a morning scribble
out of inky gloss & the unwritten to the eye
in nightscriptdarkness I mouthdesire means I sea
of breath. "The unsoled of the day still". Wind
& coldwake are writing. Arbor air stretches [I march
fights back] the illusion of warmth
onto bodies & color set harlequins. They
play with the debris of sky the
rubble of grey dream themselves away and draw
from the first light
I see-through hiding-place

morning out of glass / I mirror morning

zweizeiler am 19. 04. 2002

ein kiebitz spreizt das ohr. Im frühen ruf
sickern nacht aus dem coyotenkopf & nebelruderer

two-liner on April 19, 2002

                    a pewit spreads the ear. In the early call
        night trickling out of the coyote's head & oarsmen in the fog

hungerperspektive, Newbury Street

flaumzitterbild :
schält sonnenhaut I spatz
ins fußrevier der
federt ab neu gier pikante &
gefräßigkeit tippelt
I asphaltgrasen vom brot
rest fällt bröselsonntag der einsamen & krumen
sinn & über
bleibsel rinnsteinstreunen zeitungs
fetzen *soundwortfransen* getrocknete
druckskulpturen der längst verschlungenen
nachrichtenschwere [*groundreport*] und handwogen
stille jetzt am nachmittag im sonntagsfilm
verdaut die nach & vorruh der woche
oder *slow-motion* der kaffeegänger
sich kopfkränzchen ganz kopf-
schlängelnder schnabelhals der spatzen-
herden zu boden & regenbogennacken der mülltauben
dazwischen [nickt eine hutdame dem stolzieren
hinterher dem gefieder] *breadrhythm*
sagst du *breadrhythm*. Ist I anderer
der brotrhythmus am textrand der stadt

hungerperspective, Newbury Street

fluffjitterimage :
peels sunskin I sparrow
into the foot district it
feathers down go rging picante &
gluttony tip taps
I asphaltgrazing from the bread-
pickings falls a smidginsunday of the lonesome & crumbled
sense & left
overs curbstone roaming paper
shreds *soundwordfrays* dried
printsculptures of the long-ravened
newsweight [*groundreport*] and handbillows
silence now in the afternoon in the sunday movie
digested the after & before stillness of the week
or *slow-motion* of the coffee goers
themselves headcups all head-
curving beakneck of the sparrow-
herds on the ground & rainbow napes of the garbage pigeons
in between [a hat lady nods toward
the prancing, the plumage] *breadrhythm*
you say *breadrhythm*. It is off-b:eat
der brotrhythmus at the textfringe of the city

ankunft in N.Y.

[I 2 3] aufgehört zu zählen
die straßen. Es gibt
die biographie
losigkeit I massenziel [Du & ich]
I reiseführer in N.Y. &

straßenstottern im kopf
zu buchstabieren
„underground" & graphisch
darstellbar die abmessung der filme
aus dem archiv
so was wie „lieb" in allen sprachen

lautgebärden vor beton

arrival in N.Y.

[1 2 3] stopped counting
the streets. There is
the biography
lessness I mass destination [You & i]
I travel guide in N.Y. &

street stammering in the head
to alphabetize
"untergrund" & graphically
presentable the movies' dimension
from the archive
something like "2 love" in all languages

soundgestures before concrete

N.Y. & sturz & stand & treibblechhaare
bettler stümpfe taillen aus
schnitt: auf aughöhweite sich erkunden die
vom zeitfall die vom lärmfallflimmern die
vom flickzitierten lichtfallflimmern
glasreflextraversen &
sichtschachtlängen im zerrflußwinkel im
vorwärtsschieben im kreiselnabel rollen
urnenuhren rundumzeiten
müllkrachleeren die vom ampeltakt gesetzten
lebensläufe wiegen gräber sonstgebaren die
in stopp & laufgesetzten skizzen [SILHOUETTEN-
LEIBER] lachen neugier
: I blickvertuschen heimlich doch & auf
geräumt das auge schließlich
aufgeräumt das auge. „Demut" – sagte Brodsky – vom
grellgespannten stromgekreuzten über unter
& geometrisch vom eckkanthimmel vom
vorn & hinten schluchtgeführten & das sich
vom massentropf verrettende im ohr &
downtowntaumel weich
ist loszuhören ist
rudelstille bald. Immerher & Immerfort bis
zur rudelstille schaubleich parallel
& jemand immer

vielleicht I mitgebrachtes selbstportrait
[LAUFPORTRAIT] der flucht
im vertriebenen / vertreibenden zigfach
der straßengitter &
SEELENZITTERN go & go

N.Y. & fall & stand & driving metal hair
beggars stumps me(a)te out
cut: at eye to eye scope to explore oneself
from falling time falling noise flicker
patchy cited light fall flickering
the glassreflextraverse &
long lines of sight shafts in
streamed distorted angles
while edging onwards rolling at the navel spinner
urnhours all around times
garbagebang voids and the traffic lights cycle setting
ways of life swaying graves elsewise conduct
sketches paused & brought into running [SILHOUETTE-
SKINS] laughter curiosity
: I gaze glossed over covert though & un
cluttered the eye after all
uncluttered the eye. "Humility" – Brodsky[124] said –
to the glaringly spanned to lines current(ly) crossed over under
& geometrically to the squareskies to
front & back shaft guided &
to the drip of masses (re)covered in the ear &
downtowntumble soft
is what is to un-listen to
is herd's silence soon. Always here & Always gone
until herd's silence visually pale parallel
& always somebody

maybe I self-portrait brought along
[RUNPORTRAIT] of escape
in the displaced / displacing manIfold
of streets after streetgrids &
SOULTREMBLING *go & go*

vom schnee

fuß & handnoten im kopfkörper
I zu klärendes winterfeld : I HERZ-
GEWAND, schwebestill. I weiß-
vertauchen / flockenlider
I schneefenster &
schlittenfahrten im gesicht

: wie wir kinder die SCHNEETRÄNEN zählten die
summe aller kindsbuchstaben. Von den fensterscheiben
ins wärmende wort & nachzeichnend
I SATZ WINTERW:ORTE &
geschichten aus dem HOLZ geborgen. Feuer
& futter / in die splittergänge der holzscheite gelegt
& trocken vor schnee

from snow

foot & handnotes in the head corpus
I winterfield ought to be cleared : I HEART-
GARMENT, float-still. I white im
mersion / flaking com/position
I snowwindow &
sled rides written on the face

: how we children counted the SNOWTEARS the
sum of all kids' alphabets. From the windowpane
into the warming word & tracing
I SET WINTERWOR(L)DS &
tales retrieved from the WOOD. Fire
& feed / laid into the logs' sliver canals
& dry with snow

unterschlupf
2006

hideaway

schwarzweiß bild ortsbe
stimmung in zustandsfarben. [sandschwarz &
sandweiß]. Der nacht-
portier die gebetskette in der hand & neben ihm
I polizist [im sommer
uniformweiß] den Koran laut-
sagend. Stadt
meditative nachmitternacht /

: uhr
zeigersprung. Wie wir aufstanden wie wir aufgestanden
wurden / ins gewitter knieten den rosenkranz
die gefalteten blicke unterm herrgottswinkel die marien-
statue kopfbedeckt

wie heuer vollmond ist & keine wolke
am himmel &

wie wir nicht verstanden das machtwort
„unheil". Nur wußten damals
daß aufgeschlagene ellbogen
& knie wundheilten. I halbmond
bild im kopfwuchs & mantelblau die ähren
hinterm kreuz den laib / das leibbrot

: uhr
zeigersprung. Wie das feilgebotene brot auf dem gehsteig
andacht wurde
und keine weitere geste [BROTBEDÜRFTIG]. Die
brotschlitten im nachhinein
HUNGERPRÄSENS / immerpräsens
& handelseinig I erdverstauben

& trage den sandschutz um den mund
SEELENSCHUTZ /

(Kairo, 2004)

230

blackandwhite image dis
position finding in inventory colors. [sandblack &
sandwhite]. The night-
porter with prayer beads in his hand & next to him
a policeman [in summer
uniformwhite] reciting the Koran
aloud. City
meditative mid-midnight /

: clock
hand leap. How we got up how we had to
get up / kneeling the rosary into the thunderstorm
folded gazes below the home-crucifix the statue
of the Virgin headscarfed

such a full moon tonite & no cloud
above &

how we did not comprehend the might in
"misery". All we knew
was that skinned elbows &
knees would heal. I half-moon
image in the head rose & rye ears in coat-blue
behind the cross the body aloof / a loaf of bread

: clock
hand leap. How the bread for sale on the sidewalk
became devotions
and no further gesture [BREADNEEDY]. The
breadtrolley by hindsight
HUNGERPRESENCE / alwayspresent &
mutually agreed upon I dust-laden ground

& wear the sand mask to protect my mouth
SOULPROTECTION /

(Cairo, 2004)

231

gedicht, nachtreibend

dort stand der leuchtturm
ertrank die entfernung

& ist der tod
I meisterschüler der see

poem, add adrift

there stood the lighthouse
drowned the distance

& is death
I master student of the sea

: sitze in einem café / ecke fuß-
gängerzone in Casablanca. Dumpfe
ohren körperdumpf hautnackt &
empfange, lasse nicht ein
die gesten typen irgendmenschen
& doch // bin schreibspur ganz
& der sich an die rücken heftet
[innehaltende krämpfe der schritte / EILSCHRITTE,
unbeteiligt] & bin
der mit den händen spricht
& spastisch vom ohralmosen in der milde
der zögerlichen blicke & spüre
die aufdringlichkeit von tempo-
taschentüchern kaugummi kugelschreibern
auf verbissenen lippen verbissene augen
[enttäuschtes abwenden der überleben-
händler] SMOGGERAUSCH
in den fingerspitzen neben mir I "alló"
I katze in raubtierstellung taubennah
anschmiegsames räubern & über mir
die nach außen gestülpte jalousie
als müsste licht eingesammelt werden
in die absprache aus straße & heim
& am himmel ein kleiner wolkentrieb
& wie resigniert I fortsetzung
spielen 3 berber auf [geige tamburin
& tamburin] I erdiger schrei
I massengewaltiges des unbekannten
versöhnen nicht die fehlenden saiten I oud
aus dem neon stottern augen [HUPAUG]
& I behören - I behören des taumels / STAUB
TAUMEL & alle gebete sind fern
ich weiche aus
: I sammeltaxi lang übersicht
kopfbedeckt

: I sit in a café / in Casa-
blanca corner pedestrian zone. Dampened
ears bodies-damping skinnaked &
receive, do not let in
gestures groups somepeople
& though // be a writing trace entirely
& the one who rivets on the backs
[pausing cramps of steps / HASTYSTEPS,
bystanding] & am the one
who speaks through hands
& spastic from audible alms in the mildness
of hesitant gazes & feel
the importunity of hand-
kerchiefs alias kleenex wrigley's ball pens
pressed eyes at pressed lips
[disappointed survival-
hawkers turn away] SMOGZONEBUZZ
in the fingertips next to me I "alló"
I cat in predator posture pigeonclose
cuddly preying & above me
sunblinds turned outwards
as if light must be collected into
the agreement between pavement & home
& in the sky a small clouddrive
& as if resigned I continuation
3 berbers striking up [violin tambourine
tambourine] I earthy cry
I massmassive of the unknown
don't the missing notes reconcile I oud
out of the neon stammer eyes [HONKEYE]
& I sound tapping - I t(r)apping of the TUMBLE / DUST
TUMBLE & all prayers are far
I sidestep
: I shared taxi ride long clear view
headcovered

ankommen
in der syntax der handelsmetropole GEHSTEIG

die fußwaschung vor dem gebet
& wasserglut der letzten dinge

die stumme präsenz
der almosenhand I blinder
der nicht hörte „Allah" -

das versammelte blau
der taximetapher : die wegzehr
des geldes & rosenkranzklang der münzen

I zigarettenverkäufer
die brotschmiede
das spechtklopfen des schuhputzers

& windkompaß der pappel / astkauerndes grün
= staubgrün / lauthals die einkehr
der stimmen. Orientierung & zeitmedina

die wörterhändler um benachbarte uhren
die farbgewähr der lust
& die geheimen sprachen aus schritt & handritual

I genitiv & nicht zu besitzen
die großen augen der straße

                                                    arrival
        at the syntax of the commercial metropolis SIDEWALK

                                    foot washing before the prayer
                                    & waterglow of the last things

                                            silent presence
                                    of the alms hand I blind man
                                    who did not hear "Allah"-

                                            collected blue
                                    of the taxi metaphor : pro visions
                                    of money & rosary jingle of mintage

                                            I cigarette seller
                                            the bread smith
                                    woodpecking of the shoeblack

        & windcompass of the poplar / branch-squatting green
                = dustgreen / loudish the contemp(e)lation
                        of voices. Orientation & timemedina

                    word traders around neighboring clocks
                            colorpromise of delight
        & the secret languages of footstep and handritual

                                    I genitive & not to own
                                    the giant eyes of the street

Don Quijote

nun sind die windmühlen zwerge
& hinter den ohren wächst I fleck
der keinen hufschlag mehr aufnehmen kann

nun sind die windmühlen cyberskelette
& I herrenleiter lang
auf die kannst du steigen & plastik polieren

im gras ist die blasse farbe beton
I schultafel kreide im maul
komm, lass uns die mühlen beschriften

Don Quijote

now the windmills are dwarfs
& behind the ears grows I patch
that can not take up a hoofbeat anymore

now the windmills are cyberskeletons
& I masterladder long
that you can climb up & brighten plastic

in the grass the pale color is cement
I blackboard chalk in the jaw
come with me & let us letter the mills

fahrtenschreiber
2010

tripwriter

Czernowitz

vom silber der dächer
kraucht lärm / ein laut-

fall der spatzen & verse
die sind

biographische lotsen
mediterrane matrosen

mein vogelaug streift
I meer übers land & fasst

einen lufttisch dem gast
mit heimweh gedeckt / das

sammelt sich fort
& trägt

ein paar schuhe
im hals / mein geburtsort

ein atlas
der bleibendes ist

& flickwerk der straßen &
heimatlos nah / ein

paar tage C.
verschluckt meine haut

buchenverbrämt
julidaheim

Czernowitz[125]

from the silver of the roofs
creeps noise / a sound-

fall of sparrows & verses
that are

biographical pilots
mediterranean seamen

my birdeye g(r)azes
I ocean over land & grasps

an airtable for the guest
homesickness is set / this

carries itself over
& wears

a pair of shoes
in the throat / my place of birth

an atlas
that ought to persist

& patchwork of streets &
heimatless close / a

few days C.
swallows my skin

beechembellished
julymyhome

jetzt, jetzt

von der anmut der rosen lernen
von der vernarbung der abgeernteten farben

vom dorn der würde
vom welken

vom aufatmen
& vom mund

der sich selber trinkt

learning from the grace of roses
from the scars of harvested colors

from the thorn of dignity
from withering

from yet another breath
& from a mouth

drinking itself

kurische dreizeiler

die verwischte uhr
aus dünensand und haff
ziffernblatt der see

nicht zu entschüsseln
die windgeburt der sandschrift
I grenzalphabet

gewürfeltes brot
die sprache der hoffnung
wie ebbe & flut

curonian three-liners[126]

the washed-out hour
out of dune sand and lagoon
current page to the sea

not to decipher
the windbirth of sandscript
I borderline alphabet

the diced bread
language of hope
just as ebb & flow

zu Rose Ausländer

ihr lichtalphabet, wo?
das flügelleere dichterzimmer / ich hab es
nicht gefunden / I w:ort

im buchenland vom buchenblatt
der reim eine fußnote weiter
ihr zeitmaß. Sie ging

die kellerstufen ins exil
dann folgte den asseln
das niemandhaus

& war fortan nachbewohnt
& jemand sagt: „Rück-
schmerz der Verse." Sie

knien ins wandergebet
aus mutter & sprache & geben
der nacht vielleicht einen tag

: die nächste „heimatlosigkeit"
die wohnt im menschenw:ort
& füllt die koffer mit namen

to Rose Ausländer[127]

her gleamalphabet, where?
the wingvoid room of the poet/ I haven't
found it / I wor(l)d

in the beechland from the beech leaf
the rhyme one footnote further
her meter of time. She took

the basement steps into exile
later cellar beetles
followed by a no man's home

& from here on re-occupied
& someone says: "Back-
lash pain of verses." They

kneel into the wandering prayer
out of mother & tongue & giving
maybe a day to the night

: the next "heimatlessness"
dwells in the human wor)l(d
& fills the baggage with names

[aprilvierzeiler]

im klausenröckchen schokolade
das Kreuz tropft marzipan
& schnee-
verschnitt. Vorm fenster

nistet Ostara
auf frühen kirschbaumblüten
ihr frischweiß altgeronnen
das laub ist jung. Es pokert sätze / auf-

geflaumtes grün / ein
handgemachter sonnenvierter [april-
versponnen / april-
besommert] zwingt

die blüten blütenauf / reicht
an die
lust der maialtäre. Da schreit
sich einer heimatfroh / : froh. Die wolken sind

kajütentüren. Dort
laufen leichen aus ins blau / die
kommen allesamt vom meer & sind
ganz schwarz. Die menschen-

spieler schachern eifrig
am hasentisch ums knospenweh
: I spieler setzt auf afrika, der will noch
punkten. [Zu spät]. Die edel-

hölzer sind verhandelt / die opfer-
zahlen kontingente
das exil
ist altpapier. Das wort

easter sunday, travesties

[april four-liner]

in the tavernjacket chocolate
from the Cross drips marzipan
& snow-
blend. Outside the window

Ostara is nesting
on early cherry blossoms
their freshwhite still oldclotted
the leaves are young. They gamble phrases / blo-

-omy green / a
handmade sunny fourth [of april-
spun / april-
summer shine] forces

blossoms to blossom out /
rivals the zest
of may altars. Here someone screams
himself into a cheery heimat / : cheery. The clouds are

cabin doors. There
corpses sail into the blue / all
coming from the sea & being all
all black. Life-

gamblers at the bunny table
haggle eagerly over the buds' well be
: I player bets on africa, still wanting to
score. [Too late]. The precious

timber bargained / the numbers
of casualties contingents
exile
is used paper. The word

wie ostereier
umgefärbt die sprache / krötenwörter, die
springen auf ans leben. Die
springen ab vom leben.

& sind
schon längst verdorben. Jemand
mischt "mensch & würde". Wie karten
: [1 zufalleskonjunktiv]. Das wasser

speit verdruss / gleichgültigkeit
& selbst *der Himmel*
: brache. Die Kinder
suchen nester ab. Die welt

ist kein versteck / vom hasentisch
fällt dann ein stein. Vom stein
starrt her ein engelsaug
samt schwert. Das grab / die gräber

sind im off. Der tag, 1 wurf
hortensienbälle, die nackt-
verglühen. Auch sie
im bilde / surreal

„es schwimmt sich schön im mittelmeer"

like easter eggs
re-dyed the language / toadwords, leap
ing onto life. Leaping
down from life.

& being
rotten for ages. Somebody
reshuffles "human & dignity". Like cards
: [I conditional by chance]. The water

spits displeasure / languidness
& even *Heaven*
: fallow land. Children
hunt for easter eggs. The world

no hideout / from the bunny table
later falls a stone. From the stone
an angel's eye is staring
with one s:word. The grave / the graves

stay in the *off*. The day, I throw
hydrangea balls nakedly
are burning up & are also
kept in the picture / surreal

"how lovely to swim in the mediterranean"[128]

Maria Magadalena. Wie

I brief & ungeöffnet. Leib-
horizont I liebesbrief

das zu beschrift. Ende der rotkontur
& babylonisch. Nicht

aufzulesen [I NAMENSROT I MANTEL-
ROT] I sich sanft

ergebendes. So stand sie dort
[ich sprach im rotlichtviertel vor]

& wärmendes zerfließen
im namensschleier stein & haut

die nicht
erreicht wird. Eine ahnung

im gesicht. Es bleibt I preis
I falten wurf der scheu & wird

erzählt
I lieb / die lieb-

gewähr & nackt
: vernarbte zärtlichkeit. So kaute sie das holz

& aufgehoben & geborgen
die furcht im altwort *Angesicht*

& hausen namensschatten lippen
die grabbestürzten
engel. I gebet I breit den mantel
aus & angedeutet abbruch fällt

erinnerung
& die erfindung jeder zeit

Maria Magdalena. Like

I letter & unopened. Skin
horizon I loveletter

to label the en(d)velope of red contour
& Babylonian. Un

gleanable [I NAMERED I COAT-
RED] I gently app-

earing. That's how she stood there
[I came personally to the red-light district]

& warming diffluence
at the name's veil brick & skin

not being
reached. A foreshadow

at the face. I price remains
I cr:ease turning shy & is

told
I l:ove / the love

promise & naked
: scarred tenderness. That's how she chewed the wood

& kept & save
the fear in the archaic word *face to face*

& dwelling shades of names lips
the graveangels fallen down & up
set. I prayer I Maria your coat un-
fold & hinted abruption falling

memory
& invention of all time

255

im kuss
ist ein vergessen

ist ein vergessen wieder-
holung &

each kiss
bears a neglect

bears a neglect re-
petition &

liebwill I

übersetze deine haut
auf meine / SEELEN-
TRINKE den herzschlag der gedanken
„lichtalmosen"
die ateminsel. Danach
das atoll deines namens. Übersetze
I luftholen FIEBER-
TRINKE I rund I mond I hälfte
der berührungen, schöpfend
die zeit aufbrechenden hände
immer wieder uhrenstill / eine uhrenstille zeit
wie anders könnte sie gezähmt?

transcribe your skin onto mine / SOUL-
DRINK the heartbeat of thoughts
"alms of light"
the breath island.Then
the atoll of your name. Translate
I inhaling FEVER-
DRINK I round I moon I half
of touches, at the well
hands breaking into time
ever again hourstill / an hoursilent time
how else could it be tamed?

wundgewähr
2018

woundpromise

w:orte & Hausach im ohr

1
von der überschaubarkeit das lernen
vom nachthorizont die augen
& vom tagesschatten das ohr
aber die stille
aber der baum der gewährten stille

2
was das gebälk nicht zusammenhält
das versagte der jahre
& die abgehetzten biographien
aber das wasser
aber das unsichtbare wasser im licht

3
im körberflechten
die namenlosen hände
aus alltäglichkeiten & geschichte
was die not im w:ort versammelt
das brot das wasser

4
im blütenkelch die letzte stille
die atemlosigkeiten
aus welken & w:erden
aber das licht
aber das brot das wasser sagt

wor(l)ds & Hausach echoing[129]

1
from clarity the searching
the eyes from the night horizon
& from midday shade the ear
but silence
but the tree of bestowed silence

2
what the woodwork can't hold together
lies on these years
& the rushed about biographies
but water
but the invisible water in the light

3
in basketweaving
the nameless hands
of everydays & history
what need gathers in the wor(l)d
the bread the water

4
in the blossom chalice the last silence
the breathlessness
of withering & be:come
but the light
but the bread the water says

lied haft

& öffnet sich der tag
wie die nacht sich öffnet &
öffnet sich die nacht
wie der tag sich öffnet

& wiederholen sich die tage
wie die nächte sich wiederholen &

bleibt was b:leibt, nicht

& ist I sprachlos geworfen
wie ein anker
auf zeit, hier

& öffnet sich das meer
wie das land sich öffnet &
öffnet sich das land
wie das meer sich öffnet

& wiederholen sich die meere
wie die länder sich wiederholen &

bleibt was b:leibt, nicht

& ist I sprachlos gelichtet
wie ein anker
auf zeit, dort?

& wiederholen sich die wörter
wie die sätze sich wiederholen &

verschließt sich das wort, w:ortlos

behind the bars of song

& opens the day
as the night herself opens &
opens the night
as the day opens himself

& repeated the days
as the nights themselves repeat &

stays what does (not) st|ay

& is one tongue-tide thrown
like an anchor
for now, here

& opens the ocean
as the land itself opens &
opens the land
as the ocean opens himself

& repeated the oceans
as the lands themselves repeat

stays what does (not) st|ay

& is one tongue-tide weighed
like an anchor
for now, there?

& repeated the words
as the sentences themselves repeat &

seals itself the word, wor(l)dless

seelenlichtbrücken

von fried & machern sei die rede
& vom erhoffen

gem:einsame w:orte
erzählen

I stetes entnarben, seelen
lichtstrahlen

die wegzehr heißt durst
. I lebensmotiv

& wirwund die unruh, das sehnen
wie brücken

aus nicht-wort & wort die bedeutung
verleibend

& immer & anders die gründe
nachschöpfend

: I Ich & I Du & flusswärts
das auge

nicht einfach nur summe aus I + I
der wege & ziele

im hören & sagen das mundohr
ist haltung

den todesgrimassen die maske zu nehmen
erfühlend

die weite der nähe ins ferne erspuren
& horchend

soullightbridges

let's talk about peace & makers
& our hope

shared but lone wor(l)ds
will be told

I constant de-scarring, soul
light in rays

the rations' name: thirst
I motive for life

& we:wound the disquiet, the yearning
like bridges

from non-word & word the meaning
em:bodied

& always & different the reasons
drawn later on

: I Me & You & down:stream
the eye

not only result of I + I
of paths & arrivals

by hearing & saying your mouth:ear
is stance

lifting the mask from death grimaces
by feel

seeking the range of closeness from di:stance
& listen

die stille berühren wie erdhorizonte
das kopfherz vernehmend

: es braucht immer 2, die ufer zu reichen
eins & einander

im zuspruch der schritte den zweiklang
enträtselnd

den mut, das vertrauen, die ufer
als hände

von ort & von ort als atem
gefährten

aus wider & ständen entworfen
die stete bereitschaft

das Ich zu benennen & fremd
wieder du

zu sagen & gehen & w:erden
& I zu sein

to touch silence as ear:th horizons
catching your head heart

: it always takes 2 reaching the shores
one & another

accepting the steps to unravel
twin tunes

the courage, the trust, the shores
will be hands

from place & from place as breath
companions

again:st& creating
a continuous will

to name the Me & foreign-
again You

to say & go & be:come
& to be I

heimweh I

habe mir
einen notgroschen zur fremde gewählt
die stiefel vors haus gestellt
& dem regen die fenster geöffnet
der wind sprach mit einem rucksack vor
am maulbeerbaum lehnte der letzte sommer
& der küchentisch ist seither gedeckt :
das erste glas wein
der letzte frühstücksteller
& sätze
die du nicht ausgesprochen

homesick I

I have taken
raining day savings as my outland
placed the boots in front of the house
& opened the windows for the rain
the wind with a backpack called on
against a mulberry tree leaned the last summer
& since then the kitchen table is set:
the first glass of wine
the last breakfast plate
& sentences
you did not put into words

List of original sources

José F. A. Oliver, *Auf-Bruch*. Berlin: Das Arabische Buch, 1987.

————, *Heimatt und andere fossile Träume*. Berlin: Das Arabische Buch, 1989.

————, *Weil ich dieses Land liebe*. Berlin: Das Arabische Buch, 1991.

————, *Vater unser in Lima*. Tübingen: Heliopolis Verlag, 1991.

————, *Gastling*. Berlin: Das Arabische Buch, 1993.

————, *Austernfischer, Marinero, Vogelfrau: Liebesgedichte und andere Miniaturen*. Berlin: Das Arabische Buch, 1997.

————, *fernlautmetz*. Frankfurt/M.: Suhrkamp Verlag, 2000.

————, *nachtrandspuren*. Frankfurt/M.: Suhrkamp Verlag, 2002.

————, *finnischer wintervorrat*. Frankfurt/M.: Suhrkamp Verlag, 2005.

————, *unterschlupf*. Frankfurt/M.: Suhrkamp Verlag, 2006.

————, *fahrtenschreiber*. Frankfurt/M.: Suhrkamp Verlag, 2010.

————, *wundgewähr*. Berlin: Matthes & Seitz Verlag, 2018.

Endnotes

1 „An meiner Wiege zwei Welten, in mir zwei Welten" (José F.A. Oliver, *Heimatt und andere fossile Träume* [Berlin: Das Arabische Buch, 1989], 8.) All translations in this introduction are by Marc James Mueller.
2 Original title: *Heimatt und andere fossile Träume*.
3 Ibid.
4 José F.A. Oliver, *Mein andalusisches Schwarzwalddorf. Essays*, (Frankfurt/ M.: Suhrkamp, 2007), 18.
5 Oliver, *Schwarzwalddorf*, 26f.
6 Oliver, *Schwarzwalddorf*, 26f.
7 Oliver, *Schwarzwalddorf*, 26f..
8 Oliver, *Schwarzwalddorf*, 23.
9 Oliver, *Schwarzwalddorf*, 27.
10 José F.A. Oliver, *Fremdenzimmer. Essays*, (Frankfurt/ M.: weissbooks, 2015), 87.
11 Leslie A. Adelson, "Against Between—Ein Manifest gegen das Dazwischen," *TEXT + KRITIK IX: Literatur und Migration* (2006): 36. Adelson generally refers here to migrant writing that transgresses borders of history, knowledge and reality.
12 Oliver, *Schwarzwalddorf*, 54.
13 For example in: José F.A. Oliver, *Austernfischer, Marinero, Vogelfrau*, (Berlin: Das Arabische Buch, 1997), 8.
14 Oliver, *Austernfischer*, 60f.
15 Ibid.
16 Andreas Blödorn, „Nie da sein wo man ist. ‚Unterwegs-Sein' in der transkulturellen Gegenwartslyrik," *TEXT + KRITIK IX: Literatur und Migration* (2006): 135.
17 Fritz J. Raddatz, „In mir zwei Welten," *Die Zeit*, June 24, 1994, 44.
18 Joachim Sartorius, „Das schlanke Brustweiß einer Möwendame," *Süddeutsche Zeitung*, November 14, 2005.
19 Raddatz, „In mir zwei Welten," 44.
20 cited in: Carmine Chiellino, „Eine Literatur des Konsens und der Autonomie—Für eine Topographie der Stimmen," in *Interkulturelle Literatur in Deutschland. Ein Handbuch*, ed. Carmine Chielino (Stuttgart: Metzler, 2000), 51.
21 Ibid.
22 Russell King, John Connell and Paul White, eds., *Writing Across Worlds. Literature and Migration* (New York: Routledge, 1995), 41.
23 Ibid.
24 Today, more than 30 families who migrated from Málaga still reside in Hausach.
25 Oliver, *Schwarzwalddorf*, 38.
26 Chiellino, *Autonomie*, 54.
27 Oliver, *Schwarzwalddorf*, 96f.
28 Oliver, *Schwarzwalddorf*, 97.
29 Oliver, *Schwarzwalddorf*, 101.
30 Carmine Chiellino, *Am Ufer der Fremde. Literatur und Arbeitsmigration 1870–1991*, (Stuttgart: Metzler, 1995), 290.

31 Sabine Fischer, "Franco Biondi," in *Encyclopedia of German Literature Vol 1*, ed. Matthias Konzett (Chicago: Fitzroy Dearborn, 2000), 113.

32 Biondi 1992, 99

33 Fischer, "Biondi," 112.

34 Ibid.

35 Franco Biondi and Rafik Schami, „Literatur der Betroffenen," in *Zu Hause in der Fremde. Ein bundesdeutsches Ausländer-Lesebuch*, ed. Christina Schaffernicht (Reinbeck: Rowohlt, 1981), 136-50.

36 King, *Across Worlds*, 42.

37 Fischer, "Biondi," 112.

38 King, *Across Worlds*, 43.

39 Fischer, "Biondi," 112.

40 Oliver, *Hei*matt, 11.

41 Hannelore van Ryneveld, „Im Gespräch mit José F.A. Oliver—'vielstimmig und meersprachig,'" *ACTA GERMANICA* 36 (2008): 7.

42 José F.A. Oliver, *Gastling*, (Berlin: Das Arabische Buch, 1993), 125.

43 Basler Lyrik Preis website. http://www.lyrikfestival-basel.ch/downloads/2014_lyrikpreis_mm.pdf. Accessed April 05, 2015.

44 Chiellino, *Autonomie*, 59.

45 for example in: Immacolata Amodeo, *Die Heimat heißt Babylon: zur Literatur ausländischer Autoren in der Bundesrepublik Deutschland*, (Opladen: Westdeutscher Verlag, 1996).

46 Gilles Deleuze and Félix Guattari, *Rhizom*, (Berlin: Merve, 1977).

47 Carmine Chiellino, „Interkulturalität und Literaturwissenschaft," in Chiellino, *Interkulturelle Literatur*, 390.

48 Adelson, "Against Between," 36–46.

49 Source: personal interview with the author.

50 Wolfgang Welsch, „Transkulturalität—Lebensformen nach der Auflösung der Kulturen," *Information Philosophie* 2 (1992): 5–20.

51 Wolfgang Welsch, „Was ist eigentlich Transkulturalität?," in *Hochschule als transkultureller Raum. Kultur, Bildung und Differenz in der Universität*, eds. Lucyna Darowsk and Claudia Machold (Bielefeld: transcript, 2010), 42.

52 José F.A. Oliver, *Finnischer Wintervorrat*, (Frankfurt/ M.: Suhrkamp, 2005), 84.

53 See also: Elke Sturm Trigonakis, "Global Playing in Poetry: The Texts of Juan Felipe Herrera and José F.A. Oliver as a new *Weltliteratur*," in *Transcultural Localisms. Responding to Ethnicity in a Globalized World*, ed. Yiorgos Kalogeras et. al. (Heidelberg: Universitätsverlag Winter, 2006), 36.

54 Oliver, *Hei*matt, 11.

55 Harald Weinrich, „Laudatio auf José F.A. Oliver," (2007), accessed May 12, 2014, http://web.mit.edu/course/21/21.german/www/oliverlaudatio.html.

56 Joseph Jurt, „Die Fremde als Verlust, die Fremde als Gewinn. Zu José F.A. Olivers Lyrik," in *Lebensgeschichten, Exil, Migration. Akten des 4. Kolloquiums des EUCOR-Forschungsverbunds Interkulturalität in Theorie und Praxis*, eds. Thomas Keller and Freddy Raphaël (Berlin: BWV, 2006), 246.

57 Roberto Di Bella, „'W:orte'—Poetische Ethnografie und Sprachperformanz im Werk von Yoko Tawada und José F.A. Oliver," in *Literatur—Universalie und Kulturenspezifikum. Materialien Deutsch als Fremdsprache Band 82*, eds. Andreas Kramer and Jan Röhnert (Göttingen: Universitätsverlag Göttingen, 2010), 254. Oliver's language of dynamic movement and change also "mobilizes" pertified structures in the

politcal arena as well as in the area of national literatures. (Ottmar Ette, *Zwischen-WeltenSchreiben. Literaturen ohne festen Wohnsitz*, (Berlin: Kadmos, 2005), 201.

58   Ana Ruiz, „Literatur der spanischen Minderheit," in Chiellino, *Interkulturelle Literatur*, 94.

59   Elke Sturm Trigonakis, *Comparative Cultural Studies and the New* Weltliteratur, (West Lafayette: Purdue University Press, 2013), 102.

60   *Stuttgarter Zeitung*, September 29, 2006.

61   Title of original: *Todesfuge* (written between 1944 and 1945, first published in Romanian translation in 1947).

62   Paul Celan, *Selected Poems and Prose*, trans. John Felstiner, (New York: W.W. Norton, 2001), 395.

63   Celan, *Selected Poems*, 275.

64   José F.A. Oliver, *Lyrisches Schreiben im Unterricht*, (Seelze: Klett/ Kallmeyer, 2013), 212.

65   Sturm Trigonakis, *Comparative Cultural Studies*, 101.

66   Di Bella, „"W:orte'", 250.

67   Sturm Trigonakis, *Comparative Cultural Studies*, 101.

68   see also: Sturm Trigonakis, *Comparative Cultural Studies*, 99.

69   Oliver, *Schwarzwalddorf*, 96.

70   in: José F.A. Oliver, *Auf-Bruch*, (Berlin: Das Arabische Buch, 1987), 10.

71   Erwin Walter Palm, afterword to *Rose aus Asche. Spanische und Spanisch-Amerikanische Gedichte 1900–1950*, ed. Erwin Walter Palm (Frankfurt/ M.: Suhrkamp, 1981), 143.

72   Federico García Lorca, *Collected Poems*, ed. Christopher Maurer, (New York: Farrar, Straus and Giroux, 2002), 49.

73   Christopher Maurer, introduction to *Collected Poems*, by Federico García Lorca, XL-VII.

74   Lorca, *Collected Poems*, 197.

75   Oliver, *Schwarzwalddorf*, 97.

76   Maurer, *Introduction*, XIVIII.

77   Ibid.

78   Maurer, *Introduction*, L.

79   Maurer, *Introduction*, LVIII.

80   Ibid.

81   Oliver, *Lyrisches Schreiben*, 141.

82   As an accessible example for Oliver's poetics may serve his poem "compass & twilight" from the collection *nightfringetraces* (2002) entailing many of his core poetic strategies, e.g. foreignization and deterritorialization of language and identity, or disorientation of the reader. For this poem see also: Marc James Mueller, „Zwischen Heimatt und Fremdw:ort. Über poetische Identitätsmobilität in der deutsch-spanischen Lyrik José F.A. Olivers," *Glossen 26* (2007), accessed May 5, 2015, http://www2.dickinson.edu/glossen/heft26/article26/marc-mueller26.html.

83   Jerome Rothenberg and Pierre Joris, eds., *Poems for the Millenium. Volume Two*, (Berkeley: University of California Press, 1998), 102.

84   Rothenberg, *Poems*, 301.

85   Charles Bernstein quoted in Jason Guriel, "Words Fail Him: The Poetry of Charles Bernstein," *Parnassus. Poetry in Review* Vol 33 (2015), accessed May 1, 2015, http://parnassusreview.com/archives/1791.

86   Marjorie Perloff, "A Snyntax of Contrariety," *Aerial* 9 (1997): 234–38.

87 see also: Jurt, „Die Fremde als Verlust," 245. Jurt maintains here that Oliver's hermeticism never exposes the reader to "nonsense".

88 Rothenberg, *Poems*, 625.

89 Rothenberg, *Poems*, 622.

90 Rothenberg, *Poems*, 746.

91 Rothenberg, *Poems*, 770.

92 Rothenberg, *Poems*, 772.

93 Rothenberg, *Poems*, 770.

94 Paul Celan, *Breathturn into Timestead. The Collected later Poetry*, trans. Pierre Joris, (New York: Farrar, Straus and Giroux, 2014). Also other translators of Celan's poetry into English chose to render his compounds in a similar way (for example John Felstiner).

95 Quote by Don Byrd, in: Rothenberg, *Poems*, 773.

96 Ibid.

97 Ibid.

98 Walter Benjamin, „Die Aufgabe des Übersetzers," in *Illuminationen*, (Frankfurt/ M.: Suhrkamp, 1977), 61.

99 American translator and translation theorist Lawrence Venuti introduced the dichotomy between domestication and foreignization of a translated text to the modern field of Translation Studies (Lawrence Venuti, *The Translator's Invisibility: A History of Translation*, [New York: Routledge, 1995]). Venuti considers the froreignization of a translated text as an ethical choice by the translator trying to restrain the "ethnocentric violence of translation (Venuti, *Invisibility*, 20).

100 NPD stands for "Nationaldemokratische Partei Deutschland" ("National-democratic Party of Germany"), a small right wing extremist, neofascist party that, on a regular basis, agitates agressivley against foreigners and non-ethnic Germans.

101 Harquebusier: Most common form of cavalry in Western Europe. Also part of colonial forces conquering the southern American continent from the 16th century on.

102 Alejandro Cussiánovich, Peruvian catholic priest, theologian and educator. He worked since 1964 with christian youth organizations, and started in 1976 the movement Teenagers and Working Children of Christian Workers (MANTHOC). He published several books, among them *Religious Life and the Poor* (1979). Close collaboration with Terre des Hommes (Germany) supporting children, youth, and marginalized communities in Peru based on human rights.

103 Carmine Gino Chiellino, Italian-German literary scholar, poet, essayist, editor and translator. He was born in Italy in 1946, and lives in Germany since the year 1969. Chiellino coined the term "interkulturelle Literatur" ("intercultural literature") in the German context.

104 October 3rd, 1990: "Tag der Deutschen Einheit," Day of the German Unification (German national holiday).

105 Quadriga: Chariot drawn by four horses raced in the Ancient Olympic Games, and ancient Roman contests. Modern quadriga representations, as profiles or sculptures, are often driven by the ancient goddesses Victoria (Victory) or Fama (Fame) and are symbols of triumph. Oliver refers here to the quadriga atop the Brandenburg Gate in Berlin located at the boulevard "Unter den Linden" in the heart of the city. The gate was opened 1791 and was crowned two years later with a quadriga driven by a goddess showing features of Eirene, the goddess of peace, as well as

Nike, the goddess of victory, that held a lance with a laurel wreath. However, the gate was initially called "Friedenstor" (peace gate). After the Prussian defeat in 1806, Napoleon used the gate for a triumphal procession and ordered to take its quadriga to Paris. After Napoleon's defeat in 1814, the quadriga was restored at its original location. However, the top of the goddess' lance was redesigned and displayed now a Prussian eagle and an Iron Cross with a wreath of oak leaves. Now she was a Victoria, as well as the gate was a triumphal arch representing Prussian hegemony. The Brandeburg Gate was closed in 1961 since it stood in the eastern part of divded Berlin, directly at the border between East and West. In 1958, the East-Berlin government ordered the removal of the Prussian eagle and the Iron Cross as "emblems of German-Prussian Militarism." After the Fall of the Wall and its re-opening in December 1989, the gate was again equipped with its Prussian symbols.

106 Bandoleon: Also known as "bandoneon," an accordion particularly popular in Argentina and Uruguay as part of tango ensembles.

107 Pablo Neruda (1904–1973), Chilean poet, won Nobel Prize for Literature in 1971.

108 Rafael Alberti Merello (1902–1999), Andalusian poet, member of the literary group "Generation of '27" that arose between 1923 and 1927 and sought to reconcile Spanish popular culture and folklore with classical literary tradition and avant-garde forms of art and poetry.

109 Ricardo Bada, Spanish-German essayist, translator, narrator, and critic, born 1939 in Huelva, Spain, since 1963 in Germany.

110 Crystal Night (Kristallnacht): Also known as Night of Broken Glass. Pogrom against the Jewish population throughout Nazi-Germany and Austria on 9th–10th November, 1938.

111 November 9th: Fateful date in German history. Besides the Night of Broken Glass in 1938, also the day on which the Berlin Wall fell in 1989.

112 Solingen: German city, called the "City of Blades" due to its long standing tradition in manufacturing knifes, swords and razors by renowned companies. Also known because of a May 29th, 1993 arson attack by local Neo-Nazis on a house of a Turkish family in Solingen killing two Turkish women and three Turkish girls. Chancellor Helmut Kohl's decision not to attend the funeral further escalated the controversy.

113 Siegfried: Mythical character of the Germanic saga *Nibelungenlied* (*Song of the Nibelungs*) from the 13th century; archetypical Germanic hero embodying "German" secondary virtues such as strength, invincibility, purity, and loyalty that were later embraced and abused by Nazi ideology.

114 With only a few exceptions, all English language words or phrases from the original are left unchanged in the translation.

115 Alfred Döblin (1878–1957), German novelist, essayist and doctor who had to flee Germany in 1933 because of his Jewish descent and socialist convictions. He is best know for his novel *Berlin Alexanderplatz* (1929). With "Döblins mordung" ("Döblin's murdering") Oliver also alludes to the title of Döblin's collection of short stories *Die Ermordung einer Butterblume und andere Erzählungen* (*A Dandelion Has Been Murdered and Other Stories*, 1913), a major work of German expressionism that thematizes the deindividualization of man in modernity.

116 „die traurigen Geranien" ("the Melancholy Geraniums," 1961 posthumously): Title of a collection of short stories by the German author and playwright Wolfgang Borchert (1921–1947), one of the most well known writers of the post-WWII era in Germany and the so called "Trümmerliteratur" ("Rubble Literature"). His work

circles around his experience of fascism and his time as soldier in the Wehrmacht during and after the war—e.g., in his play *Draußen vor der Tür* (*The Man Outside*, 1947).

117 Unter den Linden: major historic city boulevard in Berlin. Its western entrance is marked by the Brandenburg Gate.

118 The German name for mole ("Maulwurf") is a compound with two parts that literally translate into "mouth"("Maul-," or more colloquial "chops" or "yap") and "throw" ("-wurf"). In the context of the poem, "throwing your mouth" can be understood as using bad or abusive language. This phrase also hints towards the term "Maulheld" (loudmouth) meaning someone who is only a hero (Held) in or by words, and thus, who is no hero at all but the opposite.

119 Out of several reasons I decided to leave these German words and syllables in the translation. First, Oliver announces "die-hard *german* syllables" in the preceding line of the poem, so the reader does expect German language here. Secondly, the English-speaking audience is familiar with some of the terms stemming from Nazi jargon, such as obviously "heil," but also "end" that appears in words such as "End-sieg"("ultimate"or "final victory") or "Endlösung" ("final solution"). Some readers will also recognize the term "rampen" which closely resembles its English translation ("ramps") referring to the ramps at the train tracks in concentration camps where the arriving prisoners were "selected" into groups being fit for work, and those who were sent to the gas chambers immediately. The last term "mahl-/zeit" does not have an equivalent translation in English. It stands for an old-fashioned way to greet coworkers around lunch time cordially reminding them that now is the time ("Zeit") to have their meal ("Mahl"). Today, this greeting is quite outdated and only used by an older and/or more conservative population. Moreover, the syllable "mahl" also points to the verb "mahlen" or "zermahlen" ("to grind," "to crush") which as "time to crush" or "crushing time" can be related to the intended complete destruction of the Jewish population in Europe by the Nazi regime.

120 Oranienburger Straße: Street in central Berlin. In the 19th and early 20th centuries the main Jewish area in the German capital containing the New Synagogue (built 1859–1866), the main synagogue of the Jewish community in Berlin. During the Kristallnacht on November 9th 1938, a Nazi mob broke into the building and tried to set it on fire. However, a courageous police officer, Otto Bellgardt, dispersed the group of intruders, and allowed the fire brigade to extinguish the fire before it could spread. The New Synagogue is one of the most important landmarks of historic Jewish life and culture in Berlin today.

121 If translated the proper name "Bürgerstraße" means "Citizen Street."

122 Konstantinos Kavafis (1863–1933), Greek poet who lived in Alexandria.

123 Antonio Machado (1875–1939), Spanish poet, member of the group "Generation of '98" of politically outspoken writers and essayists active during the Spanish-American war in 1898. The group opposed the restoration of monarchy in Spain, and analyzed the reasons for the Spanish decline at the end of the 19th century. Furthermore, they sought to reorient Spanish intellectualism, literature art towards the European tradition.

124 Joseph Brodsky (1940–1996), Russian-American poet and essayist who had to leave the Soviet Union in 1973 and settled in the U.S. the same year. In 1987 he was awarded the Nobel Prize in Literature.

125 Czernowitz, city in the Ukraine, birth place of German-language poet Paul Celan.

126 Courland (Kurland): Historic and cultural region in Latvia.

127 Rose Ausländer (1901–1988), Jewish German and English language poet. She was also, like Paul Celan, born in Czernowitz, Bukovina. In 1921, she migrated to the United States, and became an U.S. citizen later. However, she lost her American citizenship in 1934 since she lived for more than three years abroad to take care of her sick mother in Czernowitz. In 1941, the occupying Nazis forced her into the Jewish ghetto of Czernowitz, where she lived for three years until the end of the Nazi occupation. She survived also by hiding inside the ghetto during the final year of the occupation. After the war, she met Paul Celan and also modernized her poetic style. With the Red Army occupying Romania, Rose Ausländer left the country once more for the U.S. and was granted American citizenship again in 1948. At this point, due to the experience of the persecution during the Nazi years, she was not able to continue to write in her mother tongue, German. However, in 1956, she resumed writing in her native language. She even moved to Germany in 1967 where she died in Düsseldorf in the year 1988.

128 Oliver refers in this poem to the growing number of refugees, mainly coming from Africa and the Middle East, who try crossing the Mediterranean to land in Europe. Only between October 2013 and September 2014 the Italian coast guard picked up more than 100,000 refugees, usually from unseaworthy, overcrowded vessels. The UN Refugee Agency estimates that in 2015, the year in which the European refugee crisis peaked, more than one million refugees made the crossing. Between 2014 and summer 2016 approx. 10,000 refugees lost their lives when attempting to reach European shores. (source: Der Tagesspiegel website. http://www.tagesspiegel.de/politik/europaeische-union-und-die-fluechtlinge-10-000-tote-seit-2014-im-mittelmeer/13701608.html. Accessed July 20, 2017.)

129 Hausach: José F.A. Oliver's hometown in the Black Forest where he was born and still lives today.